SONS ON FATHERS

SONS ON FATHERS

A Book of Men's Writing

EDITED BY

RALPH KEYES

HarperPerennial
A Division of HarperCollins*Publishers*

DESIGNED BY JOEL AVIROM

The Library of Congress has catalogued the hardcover edition
as follows:
Sons on fathers/[compiled by] Ralph Keyes. — 1st ed.
p.   cm.
Includes bibliographical references and index.
ISBN 0-06-016867-6
1. Fathers and sons—United States—Case studies.
I. Keyes, Ralph.
HQ755.85.S64   1992
306.874'2—dc20   91-58373

ISBN 0-06-092413-6 (pbk.)

93 94 95 96 97 DT/CW 10 9 8 7 6 5 4 3 2 1

For my father, Scott, and my sons, David and Scott, who have taught me about fathering.

CONTENTS

ACKNOWLEDGMENTS

I would like to acknowledge the following people for their help with this project: Greg Bernhardt, David Berry, Barbara Bullock, Bill Cumby, Rena Cumby, Reba Gordon, Judson Jerome, Steve Keyes, Richard Louv, Shelby Parkinson, Bill Phillips, Gladys Phillips, Butch Skinner, Bill Stillwell, and Anne Stillwell. Deborah Witte was invaluable in helping me locate source material. Richard Bullock was generous with his time and insights in reviewing the completed manuscript.

The staffs of public libraries in Xenia, Ohio and Block Island, Rhode Island and of the Epic Book Store in Yellow Springs, Ohio were kind enough to let me consult their patrons about this project. The librarians of the Greene County District Library in Yellow Springs were unusually helpful in locating materials needed to complete the book.

My editor, Hugh Van Dusen has been a fine source of support. Stephanie Gunning and Marilyn Small of HarperCollins gave me a good hand with permissions.

This project would never have been completed without the help, counsel and time of my wife Muriel. Her participation made this a far better book than it would otherwise have been.

INTRODUCTION

Like so many fathers in the 1950s, mine lived on the outskirts of our family. He worked a lot, traveled at times, and didn't have much to say when home. Mom was the garrulous parent. She discussed our day, put Band-Aids on our cuts, and lavished praise on our finger painting. During the summer Dad would occasionally dig out a flat old baseball glove and play catch with his three sons. Sometimes he'd drive us all to the beach. When we were little, my two brothers and I once took turns tickling my father as he dozed on the sofa. Without opening his eyes, Dad made a game of trying to catch us with a swooping hand as we screamed and giggled and dashed out of reach. But that sort of thing is rare in my memory. I just don't remember a whole lot about Dad during my childhood. To me he felt present but not accounted for.

This wasn't what I had in mind for a father. What I had in mind was a guy who took up more space. Someone who could hit home runs. Stare down the bad guys. Handy with a hammer, handy with his fists. At an age when bullies were picking on me, I wanted a model, someone to imitate when it came time to stick up for myself. I'd been hoping for Superman but had to settle for Clark Kent.

One episode stands out in my memory as an exception to Dad's mild-manneredness. When I was six or seven, we were at a museum in Chicago which had a full-sized car simulator. My older brother and I couldn't wait to try it out. But a potbellied guard brushed us aside as "too small" to use the simulator. He then helped a comely blonde get behind the wheel and showed her how to steer. My father went over and talked to the guard. Dad spoke so softly that I had trouble catching his words, but thought I heard, "There was no need for you to be rude to my children." I was shocked. My dad! Sticking up for his kids!

But that's the only such incident I can remember. Mostly I remember feeling that to be a member of my family was to be easy pickings for little Lex Luthors. With a soft-spoken father and an older brother who regularly got chased home from school by the Doyle brothers, I resolved early on to never, ever, run from a fight. And I didn't. I lost a lot of fights, but felt that I'd made the distinction clear between me and my family. This became the theme of my childhood: letting the world know that at least one of my father's sons would put up his dukes.

For a long time this approach served its purpose. I reveled in the many times a pal complimented me for not being sissy like the rest of my family. But as I got older and wanted to pick my fights more selectively, I found that I didn't know how. I still don't know how. It's counsel I wanted from my father and felt like I never got.

Our relationship picked up a bit after I started high school. Dad had an easier time talking with me once we could discuss Adlai Stevenson's presidential prospects in 1960, or the emerging civil rights movement. In time we settled into a genial relationship, but not a close one. Our chief topic of conversation was current events. Anything else I looked for from Mom.

I got a glimmer of something different when Dad's mother died during my junior year of college. His relationship with her had been difficult. My father clearly was not eager to go wrap up his mother's affairs, so I offered to give him a hand. He accepted my offer without hesitating. During our few days together in Pittsburgh, Dad reminisced about the troubled years he'd spent there sharing his mother's dark apartment. At one point he moved out, into a room at the YMCA, then spent his nights drinking in a bar across the street to numb the guilt his mother heaped on him for "deserting" her.

My grandmother was a bitterly unhappy woman. Her parents separated soon after she was born. She lost her mother at seven, and her grandparents six years later. After that Dad's mom was shunted between relatives and boarding schools because her father wouldn't take her in. Deep in a tattered trunk I found a picture of my grandmother as a girl, looking quite solemn. On the back she'd written,

At 13 I looked like this. Mrs. M. tried to get me to smile and so did the pater [her father] but I felt so lonely. Grandma had just gone, gone away for all time and I seem to be lost. Nobody seemed to care or to know. Nobody seemed to understand poor little one. This dress was blue serge and the velvet doily blue, almost black. The pater and I went shopping and this was the material we selected for one of my winter dresses. It was bright September and morning. That afternoon Grandma was stricken with paralysis and at night she had left me forever. I shall never forget this little dress. I had to go to the dressmaker alone and design it. I had begun to grow up.

The time we spent together in Pittsburgh gave me a new sense of my father. It was the closest I'd ever felt to him. That interlude suspended our rules of conduct. Afterward those rules were restored. Our conversations reverted to Eugene McCarthy's presidential prospects in 1968, and the Soviet invasion of Czechoslovakia.

After college I began to feel frustrated by this meager relationship. During the intensity of an "encounter group," I realized that the most vivid image I had of my father was of him reaching out to shake hands with me as we met, always keeping an arm's length between us. As I cogitated about where we stood with each other, I couldn't come up with much. To me we felt more like cordial boarders in a rooming house than father and son.

About this time I read Burt Prelutsky's eulogy for his father in *West* magazine. Prelutsky's tribute was brief, direct, and profoundly moving. "I didn't think I would, but I shed tears," he wrote. "I cried because he had worked too hard for too long for too little. For many years I had resented him because he had never told me he loved me; now I wept because I'd never told him." Reading these words tightened my throat. I was not alone. Prelutsky's eulogy was among the most clipped-out articles of its time. It was passed from one male hand to another, kept handy on desk tops, folded and put in wallets so that it might be pulled out and shared. My own copy went into a newly-created file folder labeled "Sons & Fathers."

The second item I put in this folder was Larry King's essay "The Old Man." This *Harper's Magazine* article was also destined to become a classic. "The Old Man was an old-fashioned father," King wrote, "one who relied on corporal punishments, biblical exhortation and a ready temper." Larry King's memoir described a more complicated relationship than did Burt Prelutsky's. But both ended up in the same place: postfuneral remorse and empathy. Men treasured these two articles as if they were vintage Mickey Mantle cards. One friend told me of writing a fan letter to King right after reading his memoir on an airplane, even though his tear-blurred vision made this hard to do.

Reading the eulogies by Prelutsky and King made me realize how eloquent men can be when writing about their fathers. Some of the best reading I've done since is portraits of fathers by sons. Perhaps this subject is just too important to sully with poses or pretense. As examples of good writing, if nothing else, I began to gather prose and poetry by sons about their fathers. During the past two decades this has been my hobby.

When I mentioned this hobby to a prominent poet, he wondered why my collection was limited to sons and fathers. Is that relationship so unique? Why not include sons on mothers? Or daughters on fathers? I can't imagine that he himself believed those relationships are equivalent. There is no doubt in my mind—or the minds of most men —that the way we feel about our fathers is singular. Although such feelings are very strong, they are seldom expressed. Athletes never mouth "Hi, Dad!" to television cameras. No biker has "Pop" tattooed on his arm. Few men ever say "I love you" to their fathers, no matter how much they yearn to. And they do yearn. "My only regret," Dwight Eisenhower wrote shortly after his father's death, "is that it was always so difficult to let him know the great depth of my affection for him."

This is true of most men. Conditioned to play our cards cagily in an imagined poker game with our father, we don't say enough to him while he's alive. Only when it's time for a eulogy do we realize that our tongues were tied not because we had too little to say, but too much; not that our feelings were too weak but that they were too strong; not that we loved our fathers too little but that we loved them too much. It is usually not until a father dies that unspoken words finally get said. "I wish I could have my father back, even for just a minute," eulogizers often conclude, "to tell him what I've just told you."

Few men are able to let a living father know how they feel about him. Yet feelings for his father can be a man's strongest. Time makes them more so. For lack of an outlet these feelings grow explosive. When thinking about their fathers, men can feel as though they're sitting on a rumbling volcano. Sensing this intensity had something to do with my drive to gather son-father writing as I once collected baseball cards. Perhaps reading about other men's fathers could make it easier to deal with our own.

The most common theme in such writing is frustration about the distance so many men feel from their fathers. "There was always a stiffness in the air between us," observed writer Adam Hochschild, in a memoir about his father, "as if we were both guests at a party and the host had gone off somewhere without introducing us." Talk between sons and fathers tends to have a strained quality. The crosscurrents can feel treacherous. They communicate through codes and symbols, glances and grunts. Or by putting words on paper that are impossible to say aloud. "My writing was about you," wrote Franz Kafka in a letter to his father, "in it I only poured out the grief I could not sigh at your breast." This emotional paralysis is not one-way. Sons can have as much trouble talking to fathers as fathers have hearing them. But many men see their fathers as too remote to allow them even to try. They can easily place themselves in the opening stanza of Louis Simpson's poem "My Father in the Night Commanding No":

My father in the night commanding No
Has work to do. Smoke issues from his lips;
   He reads in silence.
The frogs are croaking and the streetlamps glow.

When men gather to discuss common concerns, they return insistently to the emotional abyss so many feel separates them from their male parents. "Father hunger" is what some call this feeling. Much attention is currently being paid to the topic of preoccupied fathers and neglected sons. One man spoke for many when he said of his childhood: "My father would come home, tired, he gave it all at the office. He had nothing left at home."

This was similar to what I'd experienced. When I looked at my relationship with my father, I mostly saw a void. Would this gap stay unbridged forever? I hoped not. In letters I told Dad that I wanted to get to know him better. During my next visit home, he spent the first couple of days following me around the house, recounting one story after another from his childhood. There was the period during high school when he delivered scores of newspapers before sunup. Later he tried to publish stories under the pen name Winfield Scott. During Pittsburgh's 1937 flood, Dad did relief work for forty-eight hours straight before crashing on a Salvation Army cot. I had no idea why my father was telling me these stories. Finally I asked him. Dad said that he was trying to let me know him better, as I'd requested.

This clumsy rapprochement between father and son was hard on my mother. By custom she was my parents' spokesperson. Traditions die hard, and Mom was visibly unnerved by seeing her husband and second son huddled in conversations that didn't include her. She dealt with this by taking charge. "Why don't you two guys go off by yourselves?" Mom would say heartily when I came home to visit. "You know, 'father and son.' " We did anyway. Over the next few years, Dad and I talked a lot. This process was helped immeasurably by his retirement. As a city planner, my father's favorite topics of conversation had been things like regional development compacts and the need for coordinated national planning policies. Such topics interested us kids about as much as the price of rice in Siam. In retrospect, I'm not sure how much they interested him. Because within a year after he retired Dad had put his planning books in storage and begun writing poetry. This has been his principal occupation for the last fifteen years.

The change was so stark that it concerned me. Didn't my father miss the career to which he'd devoted most of his adult life? No, Dad would say. He was proud of what he'd done but happy to let it go. He'd always wanted to write poetry, but became a city planner to make a better living and—this surprised me—because it felt more "masculine" than being a poet or an English teacher.

Retirement agreed with my father. In addition to writing poetry, he toured the country with my mother and sister, took part in local politics, and spearheaded a successful drive to save his town's historic library building from the wrecker's ball. Best of all, he seemed to relax. I got the impression that my father was enjoying himself. If his career never particularly inspired me, his retirement did.

Shortly after Dad retired, I enrolled in a Dale Carnegie course to write an article about it. Our concluding assignment was to talk on a topic of general interest. My classmates ranged from a flower-shop owner through a Burger King manager to an appliance refinisher with a greasy pompadour. Most were men. I chose to talk about sons and fathers. In previous speeches I'd sometimes had trouble holding my audience's attention. Not this time. Now my listeners stayed with me from beginning to end. Afterward the appliance painter said haltingly, "You know, that stuff you were saying about your dad. I think that's something any man can understand."

In conversations with men generally, I saw how potent the subject of sons and fathers could be—a blasting cap setting off bombs of memory. Men generally are deft at sticking to safe topics of conversation: baseball, the price of corn, stock options. When talk turns to fathers, however, a hush settles over the crowd. Eyes look off as thoughts turn inward. Even the most glib talkers grow tongue-tied when discussing their fathers. On more than one occasion I've seen a man start, then stop because his throat grew too tight. Even more than sports and money, the topic of sons and fathers is a male universal.

This impressed me in my collection of son-father writing. Although its authors come from a striking variety of backgrounds—many of their themes recur. These include:

Trying to meet a father's expectations; to avoid, as Christopher Hallowell puts it, his "disapproving look"

Learning not to touch one's father affectionately; replacing hugs and kisses with manly handshakes

Sharing rites with fathers: playing ball, playing cards, driving cars

Competing with one's father, in sports especially

Trying to accomplish what one's father couldn't, either at his behest, or with his jealous resistance

Realizing gradually the terrible price our fathers paid to be "good providers"

Feeling vulnerable after a father's funeral, his coffin "one removed from my own," in the words of Roger Kahn

Coming to terms with memories of one's father in the years following his death

The pieces in this collection do not all portray difficult relationships. Some are wry: Edward Serotta on the embarrassment of driving a "practical" Nash Rambler his father bought him, or Pat Jordan about trying one last time to beat his septuagenarian father at pool. A few are fictional, such as David Plante's portrayal of a son trimming his aging father's nails. The poems strike a variety of chords, including Robert Bly's ambivalent tribute to his father at eighty-five.

The eulogies stand out for their eloquence. In the first flush of loss a torrent of dammed-up words bursts free. It is hard to read such poignant tributes to dead fathers without feeling something for our own. The essays written by sons of living fathers are a bit more circumspect; understandably. Their authors are in far greater danger. After profiling his late father in *Harper's*, Larry King noted that he'd spent years trying unsuccessfully to write about the man when he was still alive. "Goddamnit, I'm intimidated," King explained to his editor, Willie Morris. "I guess I just don't understand him well enough." Morris conceded the first point, but not the second. He was right. Two hours after his father's funeral, King told his editor, "I can write it now."

Although writing about a dead father is less risky, it can also be more frustrating. Some of the most affecting memoirs are those written by remorseful men whose fathers are no longer around to hear their son's confession. One reason that the movie *Field of Dreams* struck such a powerful chord for many men was its portrayal of a thirty-six-year-old man struggling to reach a dead father whom he now regretted alienating. A friend of mine, whose father died unreconciled with his son, told me that this was the first movie in years to make him cry. I said that hadn't been my reaction. "Is your father alive?" asked my friend. Yes he is, I responded. "Well there you go."

How men feel about their fathers is at the heart of how they feel about themselves. Yet most feel alone in their struggle to do better on both scores. This book is meant to address that concern. It is intended to help men resolve mixed feelings about their fathers. If he is alive, perhaps to do so directly. If he is not, at least to feel less isolated by reading about other men's experiences with their fathers.

The best son-father writing I've found in two decades' time is gathered here. Some authors—Bill Moyers, Lewis Grizzard, Lewis Thomas, Nicholas Gage, James Dickey, John Cheever, Jimmy Carter, Joel Grey—are better known than others. Not that it matters. As this collection illustrates, more and less prominent men alike write about their fathers with equal intensity and similar themes. Its material is organized to portray the evolution of father-son relations from reverent childhood through explosive adolescence to ambivalent adulthood and the years of reflection following a father's death. Some pieces depict a heroic struggle by sons to get square with live fathers. Others portray men trying to deal with memories of dead ones. Their common thread is an almost excruciating need to understand, forgive, and reconcile.

To understand ourselves we must first understand our fathers. Accepting ourselves means accepting him. At some point in his life, every man looks in the mirror and sees his father. I did, and it unnerved me—at first, anyway. While growing up, the cornerstone of my identity consisted of *not* being the man my father was. He was usually late, I was always prompt. Dad never fought, I often did. He was soft-spoken, I raised my voice. As the years passed, however, my guard dropped. Now I have trouble being on time. People frequently ask me to speak up. Accepting any and all invitations to fight has come to seem more stupid than manly, even though avoiding conflict puts me in danger of feeling like the chicken I'd imagined my father to be.

But Dad no longer seems to be quite the pushover I thought he was. He didn't change; my attitude did. So did my knowledge about him. In our talks I discovered that my father once traveled halfway across the country to help his sister deal with her abusive husband, first taking care to find the man's pistol, break it down, and hide the parts. On his own initiative Dad later picketed a whites-only barbershop by himself. When fired as an economics professor by Penn State, due partly to his political beliefs, he took part in a protest by students and colleagues which won him reinstatement. And in a temporary lapse from pacifism, my father was ready to kill Nazis, although his fragile six-foot, 130-pound frame kept him out of the service.

Thirty-seven years later, for our parents' fortieth wedding anniversary my brother Gene and I took my father and mother back to City Hall in Philadelphia, where they were married in 1938. Frank Rizzo, Philadelphia's ultra-conservative mayor, sent them a letter of welcome to the city and a small replica of the Liberty Bell. I'm sure Rizzo's staff mailed dozens like it every week. Nonetheless, my father wrote the mayor—with whom he could not have agreed less politically—a letter thanking him for his thoughtfulness. At one time this would have struck me as pretty lame: expressing gratitude to a Neanderthal like Rizzo for his form letter and tacky souvenir. Now it impressed me: that my father had the courtesy to thank even a political nemesis for a small gesture that had touched him.

As usual, Mom's exuberance dominated our gathering. She was happy to be with us and said so many times. Dad didn't, though he clearly felt the same way. Over the weekend both told us repeatedly how they'd courted, broken up, got back together three years later, then married almost spur-of-the-moment in the Philadelphia mayor's chambers.

Dad and I were at Mom's bedside when she died two years after their fortieth anniversary. Smoking cigarettes for over half a century led to her death from lung cancer. My father was devastated. Then and since, Dad must have told me a hundred times about the day he met my mother at a meeting he was chairing of Penn State's Liberal Club and finding the electricity so strong that he could barely stammer through his duties. As Dad has repeated again and again, "I fell in love with your mother that day and didn't stop for forty-two years."

Every time Dad starts to say this, however, he can't finish. His vocal chords stop working. This happens to him a lot. When talking about something he cares about deeply, at Friends Meeting for Worship, say, or while reciting his poetry, my father tends to choke up. I have the same tendency. Dad says that his father—who owned a sand and gravel business—did too. He thinks it might be a genetic trait. Perhaps it is.

As much as I miss my mother, the best years of my relationship with my father have been the ones since she died. Partly this is because we now could talk directly, with no intermediary. Partly it's because without Mom's effervescent personality as a buffer, Dad became more outgoing. He made friends (his "in-group" Dad called them). He began to date. He bought a statue of a nude man and woman embracing and displayed it prominently in the living room of his apartment. He began to give poetry readings, buying a microphone-equipped boom box with which to practice.

As Dad grew older, it became easier for us to talk. It

turns out that my father has a lot to say. Or perhaps I'm just listening better. Dad tells me how his own absentee father was kicked out of the house by his mother when he was four. He and his sister saw their father only sporadically after that, usually in hotel lobbies. Though he grew close to his father in later years, Dad says he could never quite shake his mother's "programming" of him to hate her ex-husband. She was a difficult woman. My father has told me often about the night he was awakened by his mother who was pretending to be a policeman come to take her four-year-old to jail for throwing a cow pie at a friend. A few years later she bade her son farewell as he left for Boy Scout camp with a tongue-lashing that left him weeping on a friend's shoulder during much of the train ride.

Since his mother never worked outside their home, my father grew up in virtual poverty. His grandfather refused to lend him money for college on the grounds that young men should make their own way in life. Dad did. He got through college by waiting on tables, stoking furnaces, framing pictures, and selling books. In his early twenties my father hitchhiked around Pennsylvania and West Virginia, checking into hotels knowing he could only pay his bill if he sold some books. While he earned his Ph.D. during the Depression, Dad and Mom lived on what was left from the ninety dollars a month he was paid as a graduate assistant after they'd sent much of this money to their mothers.

As I learned more about him, I began to see my father differently. I noticed the devotion of his friends, men and women of all ages. "Your dad is one of my favorites," the man who handles his medical claims once told me. "Did you know that he wrote a poem for me?" His friends see something in my father I have sometimes overlooked: not just a gentle good nature but integrity to the bone. In time my own perspective has changed. The mildness I'd mistaken for passivity has come to look more like quiet self-possession. My father is a basically uncomplicated person. There is no difference that I can detect between his inner and outer self. He has difficulty sustaining a conversation with his grandchildren just as he had trouble talking with his children. Kid talk is not my father's strong suit. This is part of his integrity. He talks the same way to everyone. Dad does nothing for effect, partly because this would violate his sense of honor, partly because he just doesn't know how. He lacks guile. I wish that were more true of me. I have different faces for different situations, and have cut ethical corners. Someone once asked me what type of man my father was. Without thinking I responded, "He's high quality. I wish I had half his quality."

Our relationship has grown easier over the years. By now it feels like friendship. Dad calls me to discuss his poetry, what kind of car to buy, and whether or not he should remarry. When together we sometimes just sit quietly. There are few people in the world with whom I'm that comfortable. Although Dad was always taller than me, he's shrunk in recent years and we now share clothes. The first time he passed along some undershirts to me, it felt good to wear them—both the idea and the fit. We are still not too good at hugs and kisses and "I love you's," but we do the best that we can do.

The key to our current relationship lies in my father's genes. The fact that he's lived to the age of eighty-one has allowed us to navigate perilous seas and end up—him old, me middle-aged—as close companions on a safe shore. For the past few years Dad has had bladder cancer. Rather than let this disease take its course or limit himself to a single treatment approach, he has sought various opinions, tried different therapies. At one point Dad contacted a friend at the National Institutes of Health and became a candidate for experimental treatment there. Although he wasn't accepted, I admired the spirit of his attempt. It seemed that my father was trying both to increase his odds of survival and to make his illness have meaning for others.

It turns out that my father *is* the model I always wanted. When talking to my own two sons I often hear his voice emerge. "If something's worth doing, it's worth doing right," Dad tells them through me. Or, "Come on, push like you meant it," when putting on their shoes. Following his lead, I don't deny myself the last piece of candy for my children's sake, with bills for self-sacrifice coming due later. And I hear echoes of my younger self when my twelve-year-old moans that his father sure can be *boring*.

Reading what sons have to say about their fathers has made me wonder what my own might write about me. That sort of question is hard to avoid when reading sons on fathers. Hopefully, sharing other men's experiences with their fathers will make it less difficult to deal with our own. Reconciliation may not always be possible. Understanding is.

1

Daddy

LEWIS GRIZZARD / ROBERT DRAKE
PATRICK HEMINGWAY / JAMES C. HEFLEY
JIM SANDERSON / HARRY CREWS
THEODORE ROETHKE / LEWIS THOMAS
EDMUND GOSSE / CHRISTOPHER HALLOWELL
JOSEPH MASTRANGELO / JERRY SMITH

They say my daddy spoiled me from the very first day. He was an athletic officer at Benning when I was born.

"You weren't three weeks old, and he had you on his lap while he was coaching a basketball game," my mother has said, laughing now.

"He would walk around the post with you in his arms and stop everybody he saw to show them his son. He even took you with us to an Officers' Club dance soon after I got out of the hospital.

"When the band took a break, everybody wanted Lewis to play the piano and sing. He wouldn't even let me hold you while he performed. He put you on his lap and played right along. You seemed to be enjoying yourself."

My earliest memories go back to a vague remembrance that has to do with the two years we spent in Camp Chaffee, Arkansas, where Daddy was reassigned in 1948, shortly before I turned two.

I have a notion of our house there. There was a front porch, and I backed off it on my tricycle one day. There was a place Daddy enjoyed eating called The Smorgasbord. I couldn't pronounce it. I would say, "Daddy, let's go to the 'smagusbod,' " and he understood, and he would take us.

ROBERT DRAKE

Daddy would take my head, as he held me firmly between his legs, and turn it abruptly to the right, then to the left, then back to its center position while intoning:

> Look thisaway,
> Look thataway,
> See nobody coming?
> Dig! Dig! Dig!

And then he would nod my head up and down three times on that last line as though to make me agree with him, no matter what he had observed or proposed. And I would be tickled but halfway outraged too.

   Or he would bounce me on his knee and chant out an old counting-out rhyme like

> One saw
> Two saw
> Little Dicky Dan.
> Bob-tail
> Dominecker
> Deal Doy Dan.
> Isaac, Aaron
> Virgin Mary.
> Harum, scarum
> Zingum, zangum
> Bolum, buck.

And then, on the last word, he would catch me to him and hug me hard and root around on my stomach with his day-old beard that tickled me and make snorting noises as though he really, just like he said, loved me so much he was going to eat me up.

PATRICK HEMINGWAY

In the Thirties in Key West, I was a very young boy, and I think children feel things with different senses from those of grownups. Sight is an adult sense, but smells are my strongest memories of those years. The smell of mud flats at low tide, where the shore birds fed and Papa hunted; the pungent smell of a just-fired cartridge; the stale nitrogen smell of the dead barracudas as you dock at the end of a day's fishing; the refreshing smell of the deviled eggs and potato salad in the picnic lunch box.

The memories of the sense of touch are strong, too. I remember the prickly feelings of Papa's face when I kissed him good night; the warm, pleasant feeling of the yacht's deck on my stomach as I lay on it and watched Papa fighting a fish.

My father was a poor Ozark hill farmer during the early years of my life. We lived in an old log house, cradled in a mountain cove, five miles from the nearest store. Mama was busy with my little brother and twin sisters, so by necessity Daddy and I spent a lot of time together.

At four, I walked the corn furrows beside him, dropping in seed corn. When the weeds began choking the green shoots, he plowed between the rows, while I hoed around the tender plants. Came fall, and we harvested the crop together. I wasn't that much help, but I wanted to be with him. He never seemed to mind, "so long as you keep up, Son, and don't wander off into the woods."

At least twice a week he quit work early and dug worms for fishing. "You kin go," he always told me, "if you promise to set still."

Our hooks baited, his two hound dogs sleeping behind us, we sat on a flat boulder, dangling our lines into the mysterious deep. Velvety darkness stole over the blue water. Bullfrogs harrumphed from beneath willows on the far bank. Crickets and kattydids chirruped around us. Whippoorwills warbled and owls hooted. What a grand band to entertain father and son while the fish were making up their minds over our bait.

When my pole dipped, I squealed, "Daddeee!" If I couldn't pull the fish out, he gave a hand. But he always waited to see if I could do it.

Hunting was the same. Mama worried that I might fall

off a bluff or be kept out too late. Daddy only said, "If you think you kin keep up with me and the dawgs."

Off we went behind Ole Lion and Ole Muse, with Mama calling from the doorway, "Fred, don't keep James out too long."

"Oh, we'll jist go up the holler a little ways," was his standard answer. We usually went a lot further.

Take the night the dogs hit a hot trail and ran the coon far up the side of the mountain. Daddy took off running, lantern swinging, yelling, "Come on, Son," never looking back. I came crashing through the brush behind him, trying to keep the lantern light in sight.

We ran, panting, to where the dogs were baying up a tall white oak. "Hold the lantern and don't mess with my gun," he said. Then he scrambled up the tree and punched the coon out of its hole. If I had heard of Tarzan and Paul Bunyan back then, I would have ranked Daddy ahead of them.

JIM SANDERSON

One day when I was a small boy during the lean days of the Depression, my father got me up before dawn to go duck hunting. He had been a car salesman but nobody was buying De Sotos that year, so he finally found a job in a gas station. That morning he carried a shotgun he had borrowed from a friend "to shoot a little something for our table."

It was first light when we settled ourselves into the reeds at the edge of the lake. Almost immediately a wave of thirty of the big birds passed high overhead, filling the air with their haunting, unforgettable honking. I can still hear it now, when I set my memory on it. I had never seen before such majestic, purposeful birds, formed into a perfect aerial V.

I looked at my father as he uttered a little groan of awe. He stood transfixed as the flock flew across the sunrise. "Canadian snow geese," he finally said, the shotgun still at his feet.

We never saw another bird the entire morning. But driving home, Dad appeared strangely unconcerned that we were coming home empty-handed without fifty cents in our pockets. "Weren't they something?" he exulted.

HARRY CREWS

I woke up sometime in the middle of the night. An enormous and brilliant moon shone over the cotton field where I was standing, still in my gown. It was not a dream and I knew immediately that it was not a dream. I was where I thought I was, and I had come here by walking in my sleep. I came awake that night the way I always have when I've gotten up in my sleep and walked. Terrified. Terrified almost beyond terror because it had no name and was sourceless. My heart was pounding, and my gown was soaked with sweat and sticking to my freezing skin. My mouth was full of the taste of blood where I'd chewed my lips. . . .

When I got to the door, I opened it quietly and went down the hall to the little room where I knew daddy was sleeping on a pallet. It was where he often had to sleep when he came in drunk and out of control and mama would not let him into their room. He lay, still dressed, curled on the quilt spread across the floor under an open window through which bright moonlight fell. I sat down beside him and touched his face, traced the thick scar of perfect teeth on his flat high cheekbone. The air in the room was heavy with the sweet smell of bourbon whiskey. Sweat stood on his forehead and darkly stained his shirt.

"Daddy," I said. He made a small noise deep in his chest, and his eyes opened. "Daddy, I'm scared."

He pushed himself onto one elbow and put an arm around me and drew me against him. I could feel the bristle of his beard on my neck. I trembled and tried not to cry.

"Sho now," he whispered against my ear. "Everybody's scared now and then."

"I was in the cotton field," I said. "Out there."

He turned his head, and we both looked through the window at the flat white field of cotton shining under the moon.

"You was dreaming, boy," he said. "But you all right now."

"I woke up out there." Now I was crying, not making any noise, but unable to keep the tears from streaming down my face. I pushed my bare feet into the moonlight. "Look," I said. My feet and the hem of my gown were gray with the dust of the field.

He drew back and looked into my eyes, smiling. "You walked in your sleep. It ain't nothing to worry about. You probably got it from me. I'as bad to walk in my sleep when I was a boy."

The tears eased back. "You was?" I said.

"Done it a lot," he said. "Don't mean nothing."

I don't know if he was telling the truth. But hearing him say it was something that he had done and that I might have got it from him took my fear away.

"You lie down here on the pallet with your ole daddy and go to sleep. Me an you is all right. We *both* all right."

I lay down with my head on his thick arm, wrapped in the warm, sweet smell of whiskey and sweat, and was immediately asleep.

THEODORE ROETHKE

MY PAPA'S WALTZ

The whiskey on your breath
Could make a small boy dizzy;
But I hung on like death:
Such waltzing was not easy.

We romped until the pans
Slid from the kitchen shelf;
My mother's countenance
Could not unfrown itself.

The hand that held my wrist
Was battered on one knuckle;
At every step you missed
My right ear scraped a buckle.

You beat time on my head
With a palm caked hard by dirt,
Then waltzed me off to bed
Still clinging to your shirt.

LEWIS THOMAS

. . . At night, long after the family had gone to sleep, . . . my father's hardest work began. The telephone started ringing after midnight. I could hear it from my bedroom down the hall, and I could hear his voice, tired and muffled by sleep, asking for details, and then I could hear him hang up the phone in the dark; usually he would swear "Damnation," sometimes he was distressed enough to use flat-out "Damn it," or worse, "Damn"; rarely did I hear him say, in total fury, "God damn it." Then I could hear him heave out of bed, the sounds of dressing, lights on in the hall, and then his steps down the back stairs, out in the yard and into the car, and off on a house call. This happened every night at least once, sometimes three or four times.

I never learned, listening in the dark, what the calls were about. They always sounded urgent, and sometimes there were long conversations in which I could hear my father giving advice and saying he'd be in the next morning. More often he spoke briefly and then hung up and dressed. Some were for the delivery of babies. I remember that because of my mother's voice answering the phone even later at night, when he was off on his calls, saying that the doctor was out on a "confinement." But it was not all babies. Some were calls from the hospital, emergencies turning up late at night. Some were new patients in their homes, frightened by one or another sudden illness. Some were people dying in their beds, or already dead in their beds. My father must have been called out for patients who were dying or dead a great many of his late nights. . . .

My father took me along on house calls whenever I was around the house, all through my childhood. He liked company, and I liked watching him and listening to him. This must have started when I was five years old, for I remember riding in the front seat from one house to another, and back and forth from the hospital, when my father and many of the people on the streets were wearing gauze masks; it was the 1918 influenza epidemic.

One of the frequent calls which I found fascinating was at a big house on Sanford Avenue; he never parked the car in front of this house, but usually left it, and me, a block away around the corner. Later, he explained that the patient was a prominent Christian Scientist, a pillar of that church. He could perfectly well have parked in front if there had been a clearer understanding all around of what he was up to, for it was, in its way, faith healing. . . .

I'm quite sure my father always hoped I would want to become a doctor, and that must have been part of the reason for taking me along on his visits. But the general drift of his conversation was intended to make clear to me, early on, the aspect of medicine that troubled him most all through his professional life; there were so many people needing help, and so little that he could do for any of them. It was necessary for him to be available, and to make all these calls at their homes, but I was not to have the idea that he could do anything much to change the course of their illnesses. It was important to my father that I understand this; it was a central feature of the profession, and a doctor should not only be prepared for it but be even more prepared to be honest with himself about it.

It was not always easy to be honest, he said. One of his first patients, who had come to see him in his new office when he was an unknown in town, was a man complaining of grossly bloody urine. My father examined him at length, took a sample of the flawed urine, did a few other tests, and found himself without a diagnosis. To buy time enough to read up on the matter, he gave the patient a bottle of Blaud's pills, a popular iron remedy for anemia at the time, and told him to come back to the office in four days. The patient returned on the appointed day jubilant, carrying a flask of crystal-clear urine, totally cured. In the following months my father discovered that his reputation had been made by this therapeutic triumph. The word was out, all over town, that that new doctor, Thomas, had gifts beyond his own knowledge—this last because of my father's out-raged protests that his Blaud's pills could have had nothing whatever to do with recovery from bloody urine. The man had probably passed a silent kidney stone and that was all there was to it, said my father. But he had already gained the reputation of a healer, and it grew through all the years of his practice, and there was nothing he could do about it.

EDMUND GOSSE

. . . My mother always deferred to my father, and in his absence spoke of him to me, as if he were all-wise. I confused him in some sense with God; at all events I believed that my father knew everything and saw everything. One morning in my sixth year, my mother and I were alone . . . when my father came in and announced some fact to us. I was standing on the rug gazing at him and when he made this statement I remember turning quickly, in embarrassment, and looking into the fire. The shock to me was as that of a thunderbolt, for what my father had said *was not true.* My mother and I, who had been present at the trifling incident, were aware that it had not happened exactly as it had been reported to him. My mother gently told him so, and he accepted the correction. Nothing could possibly have been more trifling to my parents, but to me it meant an epoch. Here was the appalling discovery, never suspected before, that my father was not as God, and did not know everything. The shock was not caused by any suspicion that he was not telling the truth, as it appeared to him, but by the awful proof that he was not, as I had supposed, omniscient.

CHRISTOPHER HALLOWELL

When I was six or seven, my father started me off on carpentry by teaching me how to build a wooden box. "If you can't build a box square," he told me, "you can't build anything." We went to the local lumberyard and bought some cedar planks, soft and easily worked wood. The box was to be the size of a shoebox. He taught me how to join the edges in a strong bond and how to cut the top for a perfect fit. But the box was far from perfect. Though every joint looked true and tight and all the angles were ninety degrees, the box rocked back and forth as if it had an invisible fulcrum beneath it. I planed and sanded the bottom, but it still rocked, and the more I worked on it, the worse the imbalance grew. Nevertheless, I was proud of my work. I wanted to take it to my bedroom and fill it with treasures. But every time my father examined it, he scowled and said, "You didn't get something square. You will never be a good builder unless you can get everything square." At last he gave up scowling and never said anything more about the box. I kept odds and ends in it for years, feeling a certain affection for it each time I lifted the top, although never far away was a picture of my father's disapproving look.

JOSEPH MASTRANGELO

I guess I must have been about seven or eight when my father and I first became aware of each other. At the time, I was having a very tough time in the second grade and he was taking the side of the nuns who were making it tough.

"Nobody likes a wise guy," were his words of advice during a period when more sympathetic words were needed.

My communication with my father after that became a series of one-liners like, "Take out the garbage," or "Fill the oil bottle." . . .

Out there in our neighborhood was a tough bully who beat up at least one kid a day and sometimes two.

One day it was my turn to get banged around when I caught a short pop fly ball that he thought should have dropped so he could call it a home run.

Still holding the bat, he headed for me in the outfield.

I was always pretty fast, faster than that lumbering oaf, so I turned and headed for a real home run with everyone in pursuit.

Banging through the back screen door (even in hot pursuit we were never allowed to use the front), I almost knocked down my father as he was headed out to the backyard to see what all the yelling was about.

"What's going on?" (It was another one-liner he used on me a lot.)

If I had known what the word "sacrificial" meant, I would have said, "My friends want me to be the sacrificial lamb today for the neighborhood bully, so he won't beat up one of them." But all I said was, "That blond kid out there wants to fight."

"No son of mine runs from a fight," he said, sounding like a general. "Go out and knock his block off or leave home."

. . . I guess I almost knocked the bully's block off; anyway, he ran, with me chasing him, the fickle crowd now on my side.

My father never mentioned the incident again, and I just knew it was something I was supposed to do.

JERRY SMITH

FROM THE STORY "COWBOYS"

. . . Clambering upstairs, I stomped into the bedroom. My mother's bed had already been made, the bedspread pulled tight across it. On the twin bed next to it lay my father—snoring and wrapped in the sheets like a moth in a cocoon.

Creeping cautiously to the edge of the bed, I shook his legs; he stirred slightly, then shifted his weight, mumbling something in a gruff voice that sounded like the grunt of a walrus.

"Daddy, wake up!" I said. "I have to go to school."

He propped himself up on one elbow and looked at me with one eye open and the other half-closed. His hair stood up like swamp reeds; his cheeks appeared hollower than usual. He grunted at me and slid back into the covers.

I shook him again, and this time he did not move at all. Finally I jumped on the bed (shoes and everything), bouncing on it as if it were a trampoline.

"All right, all right, Randy," he groaned. "Don't break the bed. We can't afford to buy another one."

"It's about time," I said as he heaved himself off the mattress. He stumbled toward the bathroom.

"Where are you going?" I asked, following behind him. "I planned on shaving this morning, do you mind?"

"You better hurry. I don't want to be late for school. Mrs. Hurley is the teacher I got."

"Oh yeah?" he said, splashing water on his face and taking shaving cream out of the medicine chest.

"You know what she does to the colored kids?" I said.

"What?"

"She takes their heads and bangs them into the wall."

"What, you mean she just takes their heads right off and bangs them into the wall?" He looked at me with horrified incredulity for a moment, then reached down and mussed my hair.

"She does. I'm not kidding." I pushed his hand away because I knew he was teasing, and he turned back to shaving.

For what seemed like a very long time I sat on a hamper in the corner of the bathroom and just watched. He shaved slowly, his right hand drawing the razor carefully down the left side of his face.

"Come on, Daddy," I said. "We're gonna be late."

"Nah, we won't be late," he assured me, staring into the mirror.

After he had steamed his face several times with a hot cloth, combed his hair, and put on a clean white shirt, we went downstairs to the kitchen. While I glanced nervously at the clock, he took slow sips from a cup of coffee. Finally we were ready to go. I slung my army pack (which I used as a schoolbag) over my back and led the way.

Even though I was annoyed at my father for always being so late, I was glad he walked me to school. Anybody could have his mother walk him every morning. That was nothing. A father was somebody special, somebody who appeared only on special occasions, for instance, when the parents came to school to meet the teachers. The worst thing in the world would be if my father found a job. Then I would have to go back to walking with Charlie and Howard and their mothers. They always talked too much anyway.

We had been walking at a reasonably good pace, and when we came to a red light I said, "How come you have to go job hunting?"

"Because I have to find a job to make money," he said, throwing his arm around my shoulder as we walked.

"Why?" I asked. I was aware that I was being childish.

"We have to have lots of money to buy television sets and diamond rings for your mother." I noticed a slight edge of sarcasm in his voice.

"You don't have to buy all that junk." He laughed. "All I wish is that we could go to the shore sometime."

"We'll go to the shore, Randy. Don't you worry."

"You mean it?" I said, looking up at him.

"Sure, I mean it, and I'll tell you something else. I'll teach you how to whistle."

He started whistling a tune, but when I tried, it was more like blowing out a candle.

"I can't do it," I said.

"You have to practice. That's all. Everybody has to know how to whistle."

He started whistling again as we continued on the long walk to the school. We were coming closer now. I slowed my pace, looking down at the cracks in the pavement.

"Don't tell me you're afraid of Mrs. Hurley?" my father said.

"I just wish I didn't have to go to school. I hate it." I kicked a twig in front of me and sent it scurrying into the street.

About halfway down the block from the school stood the peanut man. He was there every morning before school started, wearing his crumpled brown hat and standing behind the cardboard box containing bags of peanuts. My father looked at his watch.

"We still have a couple of minutes," he said. "We can stop and get some peanuts."

We bought two bags and sat down on the wall to eat them. As we were sitting I noticed Charlie and Howard and their mothers coming up the block. I knew they would be jealous when they saw my father and me sitting on the wall eating peanuts. On the first day of school you weren't supposed to do anything that resembled fun.

Waving to them, I made a conspicuous gesture of dipping into the bag, pulling out a handful of peanuts, and stuffing them into my mouth.

"You're gonna be late!" Charlie yelled at me, pointing an accusing finger. I didn't say anything back, since I knew they were jealous. As the two of them continued on their way they turned their heads back to get a glimpse of what I was doing. Then they disappeared into the schoolyard.

As I was finishing the last peanut in the cellophane bag I heard the ringing of the school buzzer. That meant five minutes left before school began.

"Come on, Randy," my father said, and I hopped off the wall, slung my pack over my back, and began the death march to the school building.

"You'll do okay. Just don't let Mrs. Hurley scare you."

We were standing before the gates of the schoolyard now. I wanted to say something to ease the pain of going inside; finally I did.

"Do you think maybe we can have a game of cowboys tonight?" I said shyly, looking down at my feet.

"Sure, Randy. We'll have a real good game tonight."

There was a trace of sadness in his voice, as if he were sympathizing with me, but it disappeared quickly. He reached out and mussed my hair, gave me a spank on the rear, and sent me hurrying inside the gates, galloping like a horse.

I stopped once I was inside, then turned to get a last look at him. He was waving good-by. The fear I had felt was somewhat dissipated now. At least I would have something to look forward to when I got home. . . .

When I entered the living room I threw down my schoolbag in disgust. My father, who was washing dishes in the kitchen, heard the noise and came in.

"Well, what's the matter, Randy boy?" he said, walking over to me and picking me up in the air. I hung like a dead weight in his arms, and he let me down.

"Mrs. Hurley took my pencil!" I said vehemently. I gave my schoolbag a kick that sent it skidding across the floor.

"Hey, hey!" my father said. "What's the big problem? Didn't Mrs. Hurley have her own pencil?" Enraged at him for making a joke of the whole thing, I broke away and ran upstairs. I fell on my bed and started crying.

About a half hour later my door opened. My father looked in.

"Still sulking?" he said.

I remained motionless on the bed.

"I thought you wanted to play cowboys."

With that, I perked up and sprang out of bed.

"Do you really mean it?"

"Sure, go get your guns." I dove into the wooden toy chest, which housed the toys I had accumulated over the years.

The whole incident of the morning disappeared from my mind. I rummaged feverishly through the chest for guns and hats, and after I had found them and smashed one of the hats on his head, I laid out the ground rules very thoroughly. My father would hide; I would count to ten. I had to find him and shoot him.

Our house, which was old and held numerous articles of junk, was just right for a game of cowboys—old creaking wooden staircases, an attic cluttered with hatboxes and fans that didn't work, peeling picture frames and dusty books. We even had big dark closets.

Having finished counting, I began the search. At about five-thirty—the time when my mother usually arrived home from work—I was crawling on my hands and knees toward the living room sofa. I knew my father had to be hiding behind it, because I had already searched the entire house.

Just as I was about ready to pounce on him, I heard a key turning in the front door. My mother had arrived in time to spoil the whole game. My father emerged from behind the couch, signaling a truce.

"Bang! I gotcha. You're dead!" I shouted, determined not to let the game stop at this point.

By now my mother had entered and was trying desperately to balance shopping bags on her knee.

"Walt, will you *please* give me some help!" she pleaded. But it was too late. One of the bags dropped. I could hear glass breaking. My mother let out a deep sigh of exasperation.

My father ran over to help her, but she would not let him take the other bag. She walked angrily into the kitchen, her high heels clicking noisily. My father squatted to pick up the bag she had dropped, while I stood watching with my gun dangling at my side.

I remained in the living room, but I could hear what went on when my father carried the bag into the kitchen. "I'm absolutely exhausted," my mother said. "Did you start dinner yet, Walt?"

There was no answer. Then her voice rose. "What *have* you been doing?" she said.

"I was playing cowboys with Randy," he replied. There was a silence.

"You could at least have started dinner. Did you go out at all today?"

"No, I stayed here. I read the want ads," my father said apologetically.

"It's been three weeks now," she said, and sighed again. They said nothing more.

That night we ate TV dinners; afterwards my father and I watched a cowboy movie on television. It was a good one with a lot of action and fighting. Even the commercials showed cowboys—smoking cigarettes and selling mail-order lassoes. When the show was over I had to go to bed.

My mother went to bed early that night too, but my father stayed up late watching television.

. . . Weeks dragged on, and my father could not find a job. He said things to me about a "recession" that I could not understand. My mother continued acting aloof and preoccupied, another thing I could not understand. We had enough food and clothing, of course, but we never went anywhere. They did not take me to the movies; they did not go out at night themselves. My mother scolded my father for smoking too much and for buying beer. The atmosphere was tense and unpleasant.

No longer did my father play cowboys with me, even though I continually pestered him. Now he walked me to school only infrequently. He seemed to be sleeping more and more. Sometimes when I came home from school I would find him stretched out on the living room sofa in his business suit, the pants rumpled and disheveled, the jacket in a heap on the floor.

One afternoon when I came back from school, my father was nowhere around. My mother returned home later than usual that night. She did not know where my father had gone, and when I continued to question her she said, "Randy, I told you. I don't know!"

It must have been very late that night when I heard the front door opening downstairs. For a moment I was frightened; then I realized it was probably my father. Putting on my bathrobe, I crept slowly, half asleep, down the stairs. He saw me, and I halted.

There was something odd about him. He propped himself up against the wall, and despite this, swayed slightly. His eyes, red and glazed, could hardly focus on me. He held one arm behind his back, as if concealing something from me. I resumed my descent of the staircase.

When I reached the bottom his expression turned to a bright smile. He brought his arm from behind his back, and now I could see what he had been concealing—an open whiskey bottle about half full.

"Hi there, cowboy!" he said with artificial joviality.

"I thought you were a burglar," I said.

As he moved toward me, I instinctively backed away,

even though he was still smiling. He reached out and roughed up my hair, his fingers pressing hard against my scalp.

"Whatsa matter, cowboy?" he said, breathing heavily.

"Daddy, what are you doing?" I protested, trying to wriggle away.

"Whatsa matter with you? Don't you want to play cowboys?"

"We'll wake Mommy up," I said.

"Come on, Randy. We're gonna play cowboys tonight. Not fake cowboys, real cowboys." He raised the whiskey bottle to his lips, tilted his head back and took a long drink.

"Come on," he said, leading the way from the hallway into the living room. I followed him out of a kind of apprehensive curiosity. I noticed that he was loosening his tie.

Inside the living room he stopped suddenly and turned toward me, a strange, distant look on his face, which slowly changed to one of almost meanness.

"You think you're tough enough to play real cowboys?" he demanded.

He raised the whiskey bottle to his lips again; now he was swaying as he spoke.

He began to undo his tie completely; it dangled in his hand.

"I'm gonna show you how to lasso people. You gotta know how to lasso people and tie them up."

"Cut it out, Daddy," I said, beginning to get frightened.

I moved backward slowly, but with a quick motion he seized me and spun me around, twisting my hands in back of me. I squirmed and yelled in protest, but he would not let me go. He wrapped the necktie around my wrists, pulling it tight. I could feel pins and needles running through me. "You're crazy!" I yelled as loudly as I could. Still he did not loosen the knot. I squirmed again and kicked at him.

It was when he heard my mother charging down the stairs that my father must have come to his senses. He began to untie the knot, picking at it slowly, clumsily. My mother hurried into the room just as he finished untying me. She looked horrified as she stood at the doorway, her hair flying every which way, deep black rings under her eyes.

As soon as I felt myself free I bolted away from my father and into my mother's arms, burying myself in her bathrobe. Without saying a word she began stroking my head gently. Then I turned to look at my father.

The whiskey bottle dangled from his left hand; from his right hand the necktie drooped. His face was as pale as paper, and his hands trembled. He seemed to be staring out into space.

I could tell that my mother was crying; her frame shook in an uneasy rhythm. Her hands held onto me tightly, her arms were rigid and taut. "It's all right, Mommy," I said. "We were just playing cowboys." Then I, too, began to cry.

2

Dad

RICHARD E. LAPCHICK / PETER CLARK
GARY ALLEN SLEDGE / JIMMY CARTER
JOE DAVID BELLAMY / ROBERT MEZEY
IRVING WEXLER / JAMES P. COMER
RALPH SCHOENSTEIN / LANCE MORROW

RICHARD E. LAPCHICK

My father was basketball's first giant as the six-foot-five center of the legendary Original Celtics. His playing days were followed by thirty years of coaching with St. John's and the Knicks. His won-lost record resulted in recognition, fan adulation and the respect of the media and the public. As a very young boy I didn't realize that his fame came as much from his persona as his records. The adulation and respect came largely from a recognition of his caring and compassion for others.

I wanted to make him proud of me, and I thought that if I could have become a star myself that I would somehow fulfill his needs.

Such a reading was easy to come by. All his friends and our neighbors told me that I was sure to follow in his footsteps. Christmas and birthdays brought gifts of basketballs, baseballs, mitts, golf balls and clubs. Neighborhood fathers wanted to teach me to shoot, wanted me to play with their kids in the hope that the Lapchick magic might rub off on them. As I look back to those days, and see parents' reactions today, the draw and power of the sports experience seems even stronger if more bizarre. They were doing this to me when I was five, six and seven years old. I felt such pressure from all the others. I had to be good. The only person not exerting pressure was my father. I couldn't understand how he could spend endless hours talking to me, going for walks with me, playing word games and board games with me, yet never playing basketball with me. Never even *talking* about playing basketball.

One week before my eighth birthday I contracted polio. Eyes moistened, my father carried me to the ambulance. I could feel his emotions through his trembling yet powerful arms. As sick and half-delirious as I was, this moment sealed a bond between us that can only come from total communication between father and son.

Two days later a neighbor visited the hospital. He asked my father, "Do the doctors think Richie will ever be able to play basketball again?" Not if he'll be able to walk, not if he'll be able to lead a normal life, but will he ever be able to play basketball? My father was too polite to express the revulsion he felt.

The next day he asked me if I wanted to be a basketball player. In response to my enthusiastic, "yes," he told me that all he wanted for me was to have a normal and happy life and for me to give something back to society. The realization for the first time that it was not important to him for me to be an athlete was puzzling to me at age seven. I wanted to be an athlete more than ever and would spend hours each day over the course of the next decade trying to prove that I had the talent that I never really possessed. Puzzled at seven, I recognized at seventeen that my father had given me perhaps his greatest gift on that morning in Grasslands Hospital. He freed me of the need to please him and gave me the opportunity to fulfill myself.

PETER CLARK

Time and again, relatives had told me, "You should have seen your dad play ball in Monterey. He was as graceful as DiMaggio. He was beautiful to watch."

All young kids want to believe such stories about their dads. Problem was I never had seen my dad play ball. In fact, I hardly knew my dad. He had served in World War II and the Korean War and a lot of time in hospitals.

The diagnosis: He was allergic to his own body, which essentially was attacking him every day of his life.

I remember answering a doorbell in the early '50s, and on the porch stood my dad, just returned from another long stay at the hospital. I don't remember how he got home. All I remember is that he didn't seem like a member of our family.

My brother and I were mama's boys, not sissies by any means, but we idolized our mom. Our dad was almost a stranger to us.

Doctors told my dad he never could work again. He tried, but soon he became the househusband and we lived off my mother's earnings as an elementary school principal.

My mom told my brother and me then: "Dad won't live much longer."

Somewhere around June of 1955, Parker Elementary School scheduled its annual fathers-sons softball game. We had won our league easily, and my teammates were looking forward to trouncing the fathers.

However, I was looking forward to something else.

"Dad," I said, "could you play in the game?"

"Pete, you know how much I would love to play, but your mom and the doctors would kill me if I did," he said. "If I played, I'll end up back in the hospital."

I understood, sort of, but I couldn't hide my disappointment. I had grown to hate his terrible disease.

On the day of the game, while we were taking fielding practice, I spotted my dad walking through the gate. I ran up to him, and he said, "I'll take one at-bat. Maybe they'll let me lead off in the first inning. But don't tell mom."

My dad did lead off. Left-handed. I didn't even know he batted left-handed because he did everything else with his right hand. As the first pitch was delivered, I held my breath in center field. Finally . . . my dad . . . on a baseball field. Could he really play the game like DiMaggio?

He smoothly strode into the ball and hit a long home run over the right-field fence. Tears flooded my eyes as he trotted around the bases.

My dad ended up playing the whole game. He hit three homers left-handed and two doubles right-handed. He played shortstop and center field with effortless grace. He was beautiful to watch.

Dad spent the next six months in Kaiser Hospital. He paid a huge price to satisfy his older son's curiosity. His doctors were furious. My mom, as kind and gentle a woman as God ever created, even showed a touch of anger.

"Peter, you must never ask your father to do that again," she said. "You could have killed him."

"But, mom," I replied, "you should have seen dad. You would have been so proud of him."

"I am proud of your dad," she replied, "but not because he's a good athlete. He's a wonderful person. Some day you and your brother will realize that."

GARY ALLEN SLEDGE

Pooch was my father's dog, a big, happy, flop-eared mongrel. She wore clown patches of tan and brown on her coat of short, white hair, and was tall enough to meet me nose to wet nose. My father loved Pooch for some improbable promise he saw in her. I saw only trouble.

Pooch was clumsy as an ox and exuberantly affectionate. I had to dodge and weave to avoid her kisses. She outweighed me by ten pounds, and sometimes she knocked me down. As an eight-year-old, I found such behavior unseemly.

That summer it was my job to take care of Pooch, since Dad was away during the week at "the Mountain," his sawmill on two hundred acres of redwood and pine above the Russian River on the northern California coast. Mom and I stayed in Antioch in the San Joaquin delta because she didn't want me "growing up lonely and wild in the forest."

Dad wore an old, brown Stetson, and with one side of the oily brim cocked over his eye, he had the sharp, don't-talk-back-to-me look of Humphrey Bogart in *High Sierra*. I was not a little afraid of him.

"You mind your mother," he'd warn me before leaving for the Mountain every Monday morning.

"Yes, sir."

"You water the lawn, hear, every day. Cut it on Wednesday."

"Yes, sir."

"And knock them little almond trees in the back. And

Pooch needs good scraps, some of them dog biscuits for her teeth and a good run morning and night." A good run with Pooch was like being dragged by a runaway steamroller.

"You're the man of the house, understand?" I said I did, but I didn't quite see how spending valuable summer hours picking up almonds and feeding his dish-faced, loose-boweled dog meant I was the man of the house.

Pooch always made the most of Dad's leave-takings, dancing around his legs, tail beating like a thick rope against a flagpole in her eager, woeful good-by. Dad would kneel to receive her kisses while he scratched her ears. I thought it was disgusting to be kissed by a sloppy dog.

My father and I regarded each other across a gulf in those days—that awkward, silent space males put between themselves about matters as soul-simple as love and fear. Dad had grown up quick and tough, making his own way in the world, never asking a penny from anyone. He worked his way from Dust Bowl Oklahoma to California, met and married my mother when he was eighteen and then was called up to war.

I was born a few months after he shipped out to Saipan, and I grew accustomed to being spoiled by a tight maternal clan of mother, grandmother and a half-dozen aunts. My father's return when I was almost three disrupted that.

In some ways, we failed to live up to one another's expectations. He wanted a rough-and-tumble son who could fish and hunt, while I was a bookworm who wanted a father to hold me in his lap and read to me. Taking care of Pooch was his attempt to toughen me up and teach me responsibility. I resented the task.

Dad claimed that someday when he had time, he was going to train her. But the one time he took Pooch duck hunting, she came back with her tail drooping and a look of mortal humiliation on her sad-eyed face. It seemed that at the blast of the shotgun Pooch had hunkered down and begun to whine and shake. Still, Dad did not give up on her. "That dog has *ex-cep-tion-al* intelligence," he was fond of saying. "All I got to do is teach her discipline and self-control."

Pooch lived in a big doghouse that Dad had built of scrap wood behind a chicken-wire fence in our backyard. I hated going into those dung-marked grounds to feed that dog. Every morning I'd try to sneak in and get her water dish while she was sleeping. Only she was never sleeping. Out she'd jump, tail thumping, foot in the dish, paws on my chest.

Inevitably she'd bound for the gate before I could close it, for Pooch loved freedom more than anything. Then it was at least a ten-minute chase around the yard. Boy, could she run!

Sometimes Pooch would vault over our five-foot-tall wooden fence, reverse gears and come bouncing back. She'd keep that up—tongue flopping and tail stretched arrow-straight—until she was out of breath. It was hard to have much respect for that dumb dog.

When Dad was home, he looked tired and anxious. I had some hazy idea that money was the problem, and the mill was not making much of it. Late Sunday nights, after a full weekend of work around the house, Mom and Dad would sit at the dining-room table with worried looks on their faces, a stack of yellow bills and a black checkbook in front of them. Monday morning early, Dad would pack up his duffel bag, kiss Mom and start back for the sawmill.

Late in August Dad took Mom and me up to the Mountain for a couple of weeks' vacation. Because there was no way to take Pooch that far in our car, Dad asked one of his hunting buddies, a man with some country-sounding name like Claggert, to care for Pooch.

Claggert's house looked like something out of a Ma and Pa Kettle movie: unpainted, a ramshackle porch, an old car up on blocks, and a bunch of kids running around barefoot. The youngest child was about a year and a half, and there was something wrong with his legs. He lay on the porch in a box while the other kids played around him. I tried not to look at him, yet I couldn't keep from sneaking a glance.

Claggert tied Pooch's leash to a clothesline so she could run, and Dad and I left. It was hard to listen to her sorrowful howling as we drove away.

Unexpectedly, I didn't have a good time on the Mountain. Dad was too busy to take me swimming or fishing, and late at night, lying under heavy quilts, I could hear my parents whisper about "never-ending expenses" and the Forest Service demanding "cutbacks" and "fire precautions" and a "chip burner."

During the day, I'd perch on a knobby redwood burl and toss pieces of bark into a bucket. I missed my friends, and I even began to wish that Pooch was with me. At least then I could run up and down the dirt roads with someone, and we could chase squirrels and stalk deer together. At the end of two weeks, I was ready to go home.

When Dad and I drove back to the Claggerts', the whole family came out on the porch. Mrs. Claggert was holding the baby with the shriveled legs. Mr. Claggert stepped forward with one of his sons about my age. The boy had Pooch on a leash.

"Hi, Bill," Claggert said. He seemed jovial, but his eyes avoided ours. While he traded stories with my dad, I went over and patted Pooch on the head. Her big tail beat the ground, and she licked my hand. But in uncharacteristic fashion she sat politely still, as if they had taught her some manners. The kid holding her gave me a funny look.

"That dog's something," Claggert was saying. "The kids just love her. Smart! Fetch and all. Bobbie here taught Pooch to pull the little one around in a wagon."

"Yeah," Dad said, "be a good hunting dog soon as I get around to learnin' her."

Claggert cleared his throat. "You ever think of selling her, Bill?"

"No, can't say as I have."

"I give you fifty dollars for her."

I gasped. Fifty dollars was an unheard-of amount. Suddenly I was worried that Dad might take it, considering the bad times at the mill. Pooch was part of our family. You don't sell family.

"Nah," my dad said, "she's just a mongrel bitch."

"A hundred bucks."

Where would this dirt-poor Claggert get a hundred dollars? Something was wrong here. I saw a strange expression grow on Dad's face. "I don't want anything for her," he said, flat and hard. "I just want my dog."

"Give her here, Bobbie," Claggert said and shooed his son back to the porch. When my father tried to take the rope, Claggert held on.

"I'll fight you for her if I have to, Bill, but I gotta keep this dog."

My father regarded Claggert the way I'd seen him size up

a snake that he'd kick or walk around. His hands clenched. "I told you she's not for sale. Period."

"I can't give her to you, Bill," Claggert pleaded. "My wife and kids won't let me." His face was twisted with pain.

"You know my littlest got bad legs. The missus puts him out on a blanket in the front yard there, and the kids are supposed to watch him. The other day, though, the kids were playing, and the baby crawled out in the road. The missus looks out the kitchen window and sees the baby laying in a rut with a car roaring down on him! She screams. Then Pooch jumps over the fence, runs up and grabs the baby by the seat of his pants and pulls him out of the road. Sure enough, it's some drunk that skids right over where the baby was."

Claggert cleared his throat. "Pooch saved his life."

Claggert looked at my father with pleading eyes. "We love that dog. My wife makes her up a bed in the baby's room every night. We'll take care of her till the day she dies. I'll pay you any amount, Bill."

My father waited in silence, then let go of the leash. "Well, I told you I ain't selling her." He bent down and scratched Pooch behind both ears and ran his hand gently down her smooth muzzle. "So I'll give her to you."

Claggert let out an explosion of breath, took Dad's hand and pumped it up and down. He looked back at his family on the porch and, with a big smile, nodded.

"Come on," Dad said to me, and he started back down the rutted dirt road to the car.

"Why'd you give her away?" I cried, tears springing shamelessly to my eyes. "She's yours!" But I was thinking, *She's mine! I feed and water her. I take her running.*

Dad picked me up and put me on the bumper of the Ford. "Listen, son. There ain't a living thing a man can hold on to in this world unless he loves it and works for it. Those folks love Pooch better than me. By rights she belongs to them."

They don't love her better than me, my heart cried, now that it was too late.

"Come on, be big. I know what you're feeling."

He opened the car door and put me inside, up front with him.

"Yes, sir," I said, coughing back tears.

Dad got in, started the engine and then did something he rarely did. He put his arm around my shoulder, drew me close and kept me by his side all the way home.

That fall, to support his family, my father finally had to forfeit his timberland and take a job he detested in a pulp mill. But I had learned something important from him— something more important than a lesson in loss. He showed me, in a world marred by misfortune, what effort and sacrifice and generosity it takes to be a man—to hold on to the essential things and to keep safe the ones you love.

JIMMY CARTER

Before I was big enough to handle my own gun or even a BB rifle, I was serving proudly as a pickup boy for my father during the frigid hours of the winter dove shoots. Daddy would always call me long before daylight, about 4:30 A.M. sun time. Outside it was remarkably still, except for the roosters, who had often begun to crow. We carried to the truck his guns and a seat made of an empty shotgun-shell box, holding a half case of shells and some lightwood splinters. Sometimes, after ceremonially checking to be sure it was empty, he would let me carry one of the guns.

Our first stop was at a prearranged gathering place, either one of the stores downtown in Plains or perhaps a farmer's house. I'd be filled with a great excitement as we went in to gather around a potbellied stove or a warm hearth fire. Most of the time I was the only child there. There was a feeling of exclusive masculinity within the group when the men talked about hunting and laughed a lot at jokes and ribald accounts of sex adventures that they assumed I could not understand. The men drank big cups of coffee, sometimes laced with spirits, while I was offered a Coca-Cola or perhaps a cup of hot chocolate. It was at such moments that my father was most exalted in my mind. . . .

Without being told, I learned very early not to comment on Daddy's missed shots, except to phrase a quiet excuse for him. "That one swerved just as you shot, Daddy." "He was pretty far away." "I saw the feathers come out of him." "I think he went down way over yonder in those bushes."

"They're sure flying high this morning." I didn't have to do this too often, because Daddy was an experienced hunter and a good marksman; he brought down plenty of doves. . . .

When I was a child my main job was to mark where my father's birds fell and to run and pick them up when other birds were not coming in. This assignment wasn't easy if a bird was wounded but still able to run and fly short distances. Even those lying still were sometimes indistinguishable in the light-gray frostbitten grass or among empty corn shucks, which looked almost like doves with closed wings. On one memorable occasion, a redtail hawk swooped down just ahead of me and flew up with our dove. Daddy waited until it was safely away from me and then brought down both birds with a long shot. We talked about that for a long time afterwards, with my father cautioning me not to forget that ordinarily hawks do a lot of good and should not be killed. I believe that he felt somewhat guilty about shooting this one, but he never said so. . . .

After a couple of hours the shooting became more sporadic; the experienced hunters with the best stands usually had a good mess of doves by then. Most often my father and I were among the first to leave. Daddy wanted to be at his work, and after I was five years old and going to school he had to deliver me to the classroom. These were among my proudest moments: At times I would leave a few feathers casually attached to my jacket or trousers to prove that I had been hunting with my daddy. I don't remember any explanation or excuse ever being offered to the teachers for my tardiness—hunting was a routine part of life in those days.

A little later, Daddy let me use an old single-shot .410

shotgun that he had borrowed from a neighbor, and placed me on the dove field near him. Watching me carefully, he would call out a warning when a dove approached my stand and give me constructive advice after I had missed the bird. "You shot too soon." "Lead them a little more." "Let your gun keep on swinging until after you pull the trigger." "Hold your cheek firmly down on the gun stock." "Try to keep both eyes open if you can." I soon began to hit a dove every now and then, with gratifying congratulations from my father.

By the time I was ten years old I had graduated from flips, slingshots, and BB guns to own a .22 caliber Remington pump rifle and a bolt-action 4-shot model .410 shotgun from Sears, Roebuck. I was holding down my own stand on the dove fields, sometimes going with older friends even without Daddy along. . . .

By the time I was big enough to tote a real shotgun, my use of our dogs was unrestricted, because my father . . . had carefully trained me on hunting safety, proper manners, and the right way to treat each dog. With my bolt-action .410, I began to hunt by myself with just one dog at a time, usually a close-ranging setter bitch named Lady. One day, about a quarter of a mile east of our house, Lady pointed in a grove of scrub oak trees. I approached carefully, a large covey of quail flushed, and I fired somewhat blindly in the direction of the birds. One fell. This was one of my life's proudest moments. I picked up the quail and ran all the way home.

Daddy was working in the blacksmith shop, where I breathlessly described to him my great adventure. He shared my pride and then looked around and asked me: "Where's your gun?"

I had no idea. When I went back to look, I couldn't find the place where the covey had flushed. It was especially embarrassing that we had to ask several other people to help before we finally found the shotgun lying among some leaves where I had dropped it. I was thankful that my daddy never mentioned the abandoned gun again, at least to me.

JOE DAVID BELLAMY

FROM THE STORY "BLOOMVILLE"

The day my father taught me how to drive the tractor, we were alone together in a freshly plowed forty-acre field in Bloomville. He often let me sit between his knees on the front edge of the tractor seat and put my hands on the wheel and pretend to drive while his larger, surer hands did the actual steering. This day, he showed me how to make large circles with the disc attached on the back, chopping all the large clods of earth into smaller and smaller lumps. After he had done it several times, he let me sit by myself in the big tractor seat and he hung on behind and I could feel the pressure of his hand on the seat as I made a wide circle the way he had done, steering carefully and overlapping with the previous swath. After I had completed a round or two, my father stepped off the back of the tractor without my knowing it and I made one complete pass alone, thinking he was still there, and, when I looked up, I was astonished to see him standing in the field ahead of me, grinning and congratulating me.

ROBERT MEZEY

ONE SUMMER

My father coming home
from the factory
summer and still light out
the green bus at the end
of the endless street
the foul sigh
on which my father stepped down
walking slowly in the shadows
holding my hand
my father tired and frowning
eating his supper of potatoes
reading the *Bulletin*
news of the war
and columns of boxscores
my father singing lewd hymns
in his tuneless voice
stretched out full length in the tub
his calves hanging over the rim
his long penis resting
on the surface of the grey water

1 D A D

IRVING WEXLER

ELEGY FOR MY FATHER
(PART VIII)

When Friday nights are lucky, you
shout us to the kitchen table,
the smell of work still clinging
to your waiter's jacket. Lavishly,
you pour your tips, your only wages,
between the polished candlesticks.
My sisters and I, giddy with the riches,
build the coins into magic towers.
Under the flicker of Sabbath flames,
the nickels, dimes and quarters,
a once-in-a-bluemoon silver dollar,
glimmer like antique gold. "You win,"
you shout, sliding three quarters
toward us on the damask, like a croupier.
Laughing, you press the precious
coins one on each forehead.
Lean Fridays, when the money towers
are low, you grimly urge buffalo
nickels into our reluctant palms,
push your meager harvest toward the folds
of Mama's silence. An ache for you
as desolate as the space between us,
we watch you, lovelorn, reading *The Forward*,
your frogeyes looming hugely helpless
behind a heavy magnifying glass,
like some pathetic monster out of

a comic-strip fairy tale.
Suddenly a shame, a fear, a pity
is among us. What shall we do,
offer a sign of love? Hold our tongues?
In the bedroom, Mama's feet are furious
birds winging the treadle of her
Singer sewing machine.

JAMES P. COMER

A couple years after we were in our new house, I heard Dad coming up from the basement. He stopped every step to rest. He wheezed loudly with every breath. I was terrified. I was afraid that the next breath would be his last, or that he would fall. I wanted to go and help him. But Dad was a proud man. So I stood just inside the kitchen door where he couldn't see me, but close enough to rush out if necessary. When it was certain that he was going to make it, I moved away from the door so as not to embarrass him.

In those days coal for the furnace was dumped in front of the house. Again, as Dad exerted himself moving the coal back to the window of the bin, I heard the labored breathing. Norman, Charles, and I helped. Even Thelma carried a coal or two. I knew something was wrong, but I didn't want to think about it. Nobody else talked about it either, but in retrospect he knew that he was sick before we moved. He just carried on, did what he had to do, despite a gradually worsening respiratory illness. Dad was a remarkable guy—solid, responsible, caring, and tough. He was going to take care of his family even if it killed him.

And nobody pushed him around, even after he was sick. Once in the steel mill a young "dude" from Chicago who worked in the janitor's gang under Dad's supervision attacked him with a knife. Despite his poor health, Dad disarmed him with a chair and other workers had to pull him off of the young man.

When the young worker brought a grievance the union steward laughed at him, pointing out that he couldn't possibly win a case against Comer. Dad had worked very hard for many years. He was never late and never absent for twenty-five years. On the one occasion that he had car trouble near the plant, he walked there to be on time, punched in, and was allowed to go back and take care of his car. He had a rock-solid reputation for treating others fairly and with respect. The young man who brought the grievance was fired.

By the late 1940s Mom and Dad had come a long way. The steel mill had given us a small piece of the American dream that the cotton fields could not. Nonetheless, we were a long way from the dream Mom had envisioned when she was a barefoot girl in Memphis. Until now it had appeared that achieving her goals was just a matter of time. But Mom knew that the dream was in trouble, and she began to try to get a job in the steel mill. . . .

As sick as he was, Dad carried on all his activities. Mom was always concerned about the large amount of time he gave to church work. Now her concerns, abetted by her deeper fears, turned to desperate complaints: "You are going to kill yourself. Who's going to look after your family after you're gone? They are using you." One time Dad brought home the communion glasses for Mom to clean. Frustrated because she couldn't get him to decrease his church work, she shoved him as she aggressively pushed the tray back toward him. He shoved her back. That had never happened before. She was so upset she had to leave the house. Charles observed the incident and stood anxiously by the door as she left. Although very upset, she whispered to him, "I'll be back."

Every effort was made to help Dad hold the job. His foreman told him that all he had to do was show up and punch the time clock. But finally, in 1949, he had to leave the steel mill. He had severe emphysema as a result of the heat, smoke, and dust he had worked in over the years. Not only did the black workers not get the cleaner jobs—welder, machinist, and so on—they often didn't get reasonable settlements for job-related health problems. But Dad received one of the best settlements of that time, ten thousand dollars.

RALPH SCHOENSTEIN

. . . During the 1940s, every boy was supposed to think that his own father was Superman, but mine just happened to be: not a mild-mannered reporter who put on a cape in a telephone booth, but a commanding editor who could use a telephone booth to get tickets to any sold-out Broadway show. He had so much strength in just his hands that I liked to have him take Freddie's wrist between his two fingers and then squeeze it, smiling that boyish smile of his as if he were merely taking a pulse, until Freddie cried, *"Jesus, Mr. S., okay!"* Like a pint-sized fight promoter, I was constantly looking for people who wanted to trade punches with my father, a search that should have been easy, for there were thousands of liberals in my neighborhood to whom punching an editor with Hearst would have seemed like a moment on New Year's Eve.

"Hey, you wanna go shot-for-shot with my old man?" I asked a brawny boy in school one day.

"What is he, a bouncer or somethin'?" the boy replied.

"No, he edits," I said. "Shot-for-shot is just on the side. If you want, he'll do the arm you don't write with."

In my entire boyhood, I heard few lines as intoxicating as the one I heard when Freddie solemnly said to me, "Ralphie, whaddaya think would happen if your father ever hit anybody with all his might?"

"He'd kill the bastard!" I said in an orgasm of pride. "My father was a longshoreman, you know."

That was a lie: he had been a seaman; but every time I embroidered the truth, I was using my father's favorite stitch.

"A *longshoreman?*" said Freddie. "No kiddin'."

"Goddam right. A longshoreman's fists are like a fighter's, you know: they're deadly weapons."

"And they gotta be registered with the police?"

"My father could register, sure. He's just too busy catching spies for the paper."

My father's strength, achievements, and connections simply stated were impressive enough; but I had inherited his flair for hyperbole, his Hearstian touch, and so whenever I talked about him, I shoveled the shit like a circus hand.

LANCE MORROW

One Saturday . . . night, after dinner, we lit the coal-oil lamp that hung over the poker table, and my father undertook to explain to his sons how to play the game. Hughie and I were enthralled. My father liked to handle cards with a faintly satirical svelteness; he would abruptly and smoothly fan them in his hands, then with the magician's flourish of pinkies and air of elaborate innocence, he would sweep them into a neat little stack again and reach down to his pile of chips, and offer his bet to the pot in a little fluster of self-deprecation. I loved all of this. When queens showed in a hand of stud, he would chime with a sort of burlesque surprise, "What's this!? A pair of ladies!?"

That night Hughie and I learned all the hierarchies of poker, the ascending authority of pairs and three of a kind and full house and four of a kind. We learned to call the threes "treys" and the twos "deuces." We discovered that some jacks have only one eye. That aces and eights is a "dead man's hand," with a historical footnote about how Wild Bill Hickok was holding that hand the night he was killed in a saloon in Deadwood, South Dakota. . . .

As the hours of the night passed, the air in the cottage hazed and blued with the smoke from my father's Camels. The butts accumulated in white, ashy mounds in the tin-dish ashtray at his elbow. My father's cigarette smoke sometimes gave me a headache, but tonight it did not. The round poker table, the cigarette smoke, the coal-oil lamp, the chinking poker chips, the pattering card-game monologue that my father maintained ("ten-a-clubs, no help

. . . pair-a-jacks . . . dealer bets five . . ."), the sharp and faintly debauched smells of the house (spilled drinks, a bitter varnish, long saturations of cigar smoke in the furniture, something unshaven in the air of the place)—all seemed to my nine-year-old sense of manhood a ceremony of welcome into the world my father inhabited.

I loved the way he lit a cigarette: he struck the match and squinted and cupped both hands like a sailor in a high wind, like a man intently bent on performing some hasty, dangerous task upon which a great deal depended. Grace under pressure. It took only, say, three seconds, but the abrupt concentration of the act always amazed me. All thought and conversation were suspended until it was accomplished, with a smooth blue exhalation. Then the game resumed. . . .

I loved the glamour of my father's smoking. He smoked Camels, endlessly, one after another. The wondrous blue smoke that curled up from him, that swirled around him, that shot in twin jets from his nostrils or else popped from his mouth in staccato bursts as he talked after inhaling— that smoke was part of his essence. His incense. I always thought the smoke smelled lovely, when it came from his cigarette. Yet when I smoked one myself, it tasted quite different. It then became dangerously internal, part of me, a poison inside. My body hated it. But emulation was stronger than revulsion. I kept at the cigarettes and home-made cigars for months. Their allure as a prop of manhood was powerful. I saw myself as my father when I smoked.

3

My Old Man

PHILIP B. KUNHARDT, JR. / CRAIG DONEGAN
FREDERICK EXLEY / PETE HAMILL
SAMUEL OSHERSON / ROBERT HAYDEN
NICHOLAS GAGE / EDWARD SEROTTA
IVAN DOIG / MIKE HARDEN
PAUL HEMPHILL

PHILIP B. KUNHARDT, JR.

When my parents came up to visit me at school on a weekend, I would spot them way off and I would run as fast as I could and kiss them hello. Not many boys at the school kissed their fathers, I noticed, and so about my third year there, when my parents came up, I approached them slower, aware that I was being watched. I kissed my mother and then I turned to my father. He knew exactly what was going on in my mind and he waited for me to make the first move. When he saw it was not to be a hug or a kiss as it had always been before, when he saw it was to be a handshake, he smiled and put out his hand to meet mine.

CRAIG DONEGAN

Like most kids who grew up hunting in Texas, I longed to own and shoot my father's gun. By the time I was thirteen, my father and I had hunted deer through the mud, rice fields, and underbrush of Jackson County, where my father taught me how to carry a rifle, guarding against snags from wild rosebushes and the branches of saplings. He taught me about the behavior of deer during different kinds of weather and under different moons. Though I was unarmed when we hunted together, I had already shot lizards, birds, and rabbits, marking my growth as a sportsman with the guns I had owned, from BB and pellet guns to a shotgun and a .22. But I longed for the .243 Winchester that my father had retired to a leather case left on the top shelf of his clothes closet.

I had admired the gun from the first time my father ever took me hunting, and I had envied my brother when he used it to kill his first deer. Later, when my brother graduated to a much larger rifle, I saw him bring down an eight-pointer as it raced toward the brush at the end of a *sendero*. For the next two days, that shot was all we talked about.

The following year my father decided I was ready. He gave me the gun with little ceremony, calling me into the den after supper, just before I went upstairs to do my homework. Handing me the .243, he reminded me of the responsibility that went with owning such a gun and told me he would take me to shoot it on Saturday.

I gave up hunting years ago, but the gun remains a powerful symbol to me: I was just a boy then, sick with love for my first real girlfriend and angry that the football coach had stuck me on the B team. When my father gave me the .243, I knew that I had become not just a hunter but also a young man who had won his father's trust.

FREDERICK EXLEY

FROM A FAN'S NOTES

The crowd's wedge between my father and me effected its most distressing cleavage when I was a freshman in high school, playing (or not playing) junior varsity basketball. Not a starter, my vanity wouldn't allow me to believe I shouldn't be on the first team. At thirteen I was already having my abilities unfavorably compared with those of my father. Not having the stomach for such witless collations, I had for a long time wanted to quit not only that team but sports entirely. The desire became uppermost, and a matter of grievous expediency, when one night prior to the varsity game the Jayvees were scheduled to play against an old-timers' team led by my father. I got sick. My father sat on the edge of the bed and gently rubbed my head; and though we both knew why I was sick, we avoided saying as much. Gently he asked me to get up, for him; to go through this one game, for him; telling me that if I did this one thing, for him, he'd permit me to quit the team after the game. The gymnasium was packed, and the better part of the evening I sat on the bench stupefied, drifting between nausea and fear of having to go into the game. In an effort to humor the crowd, the coach ordered me in to guard my father in the waning moments of the final quarter. Nearly thirty-nine then, sweating profusely and audibly huffing from years of Camel smoking, from the center of the court and to the jubilant hilarity of the crowd, my father sank three set shots, characterized for me by a deafening *swiiisssshhhhh* of ball through net, in the less than two minutes I covered him.

After the game we walked home to Moffett Street across Hamilton Street, which was a lonely street then and settled with very few houses. The cold was fierce, the moon was bright, and the snow uttered melancholy oaths beneath our boots. In penance my father had his gloveless hand resting affectionately on my shoulder. "I'm sorry about tonight," he said. "I was lucky." But we both knew that he hadn't been; and all the way home I had had to repress an urge to weep, to sob uncontrollably, and to shout at him my humiliation and my loathing. "Oh, Jesus, Pop! *Why? Why? Why?*" I have always been sorry I didn't shout that humiliation. Had my father found the words to tell me why he so needed The Crowd, I might have saved my soul and now be a farm-implement salesman living sublimely content in Shaker Heights with my wife Marylou and six spewling brats. Neither of us knew that night that in little over a year my father would be dead from the cancer which was doubtlessly even then eating away at him. But at that moment, with his ungloved hand exposed to the fierce cold and resting familiarly on my shoulder in apology for the words he could not utter, I was wishing he were dead. Among unnumbered sins, from that damning wish I seek absolution.

PETE HAMILL

FROM *THE GIFT*

...My father's bar was Rattigan's on Eleventh Street, and it was a place where I had not gone since I was twelve, when I had been stashed in a booth in the back to drink ginger ale with a maraschino cherry and consume most of a bowl of pretzels. Rattigan's was their club: the club of the older men, my father's people, the guys who had come back from World War II, the hard drinkers, the brawlers, the guys who had been, as they said, in the country for a visit. It was across the street from where we lived, and on summer evenings, the bar sounds would roar through the nights: shouting over baseball, angry arguments over politics (they were almost all Democrats there), the boisterous entrance of wives in search of husbands, fierce resistance to outsiders, and through the nights, my father's voice.

That voice, rough-edged, sometimes harsh, drifted up to me through all those summer nights while I tried to sleep in the small room with the bunk beds that I shared with my brother Tommy. The songs were always about Ireland, about Galway Bay, and the strangers who came and tried to teach us their ways; about Patty McGinty's Goat and My Old Scalara Hat and the Night That Rafferty's Pig Ran Away; about Kevin Barry and the Bold Fenian Men, about Innisfree and Tipperary, about Irish men fighting British guns with pikes; songs of laughter, songs of the Green Glens of Antrim, where he had been born, songs of young men who had crossed oceans and chosen exile. Sometimes, in the summer, with the whole house asleep, I would crawl out onto the fire escape, and lie there—eight, ten, twelve, fourteen years old—looking down and across the avenue, looking at the Rattigan's sign hanging out over the tavern, the door open to the night, and hear my father's voice singing there, for strangers and friends, as year faded into year, all years the same, singing about some long-gone green island and his own sweet youth. Across all those summers, just once, I wanted him to sing them to me.

SAMUEL OSHERSON

Every morning around eight o'clock, my father left the house, very unhappy to be going to his store, and came back at six P.M., exhausted and angry. Angry at customers who came in every day to hassle him about prices or the quality of a job. That's what people seemed to me to do all day in the Bronx: hassle and nit pick. "Oh, the men came with the carpet but they haven't finished the job," or "Shame, this carpet's for sale two cents cheaper at Rug City." Or he would fight with business associates. He continually blamed them for his never having made the adventurous decision, never really "making it big," turning Osherson's Inc. into the multimillion-dollar business he wanted it to be. Like many men it was only later in life that he realized raising a family healthy and honorably was success enough for a man or woman. . . .

I wanted to be a friend to my father, and perhaps the deepest pain was learning that I couldn't be.

My father went to work, I went to school; we were on parallel tracks. I would drag myself to the school bus stop even as he was pulling out of the driveway to commute to the Bronx. How I hated high school! The endless memorizing of dates and facts, the narrow-minded rote and routines of the teachers, lessons that seemed so unconnected with what was important in my life, with what I needed to talk about. He had his customers with their niggling demands, I had my teachers—poetic justice. Like father, like son.

Becoming a man felt like accepting an odious burden of endless work and mindlessness. How I would have liked to talk to my father about that fate, but couldn't or wouldn't! He was so busy, so tired, so depressed, taking care of us all, bearing up so well in the arduous male world, for which my high school was merely the training ground.

Isn't that the point, though? The biggest lesson I learned from my father was that, day after day, he *endured.* You took what life gave you and you gritted it out. You were able to get the job done. And he was doing that for us, wasn't he, he took all that shit because of his wife, family, children. And is that my obligation to him? To take all the shit that life can hand out? . . .

I remember one seven o'clock in the morning on a cold winter day in the 1950s. It was time to get up to go to high school. My mother came in to wake me. I said I had a bad cold, could I stay home from school? Her friendly but questioning face. Maybe she knew I wasn't really sick, but she wasn't sure. "Well, okay," she said, and my heart leapt. But I still had to get past my father. So I had to convince us all, including myself, that I was sick. I lay in bed with my eyes closed, pretending that I was sleeping.

My father was dressed for work in his business suit and about to walk downstairs when he saw me still in bed. He came into my room. I felt a terrible dread inside me. I didn't want to talk to him. I couldn't deal with him. He came to the side of my bed. I didn't even open my eyes but acted as if I were asleep. He put his hand on my forehead. Fair enough—sick son, let's see if he has a temperature. Still I didn't stir. I didn't want him to tell me to get up and go to school.

His hand rested on my forehead like a weight. How ridiculous my act was. How could I still be asleep with his hand pressing my head into the pillow like that! I would *not* deal with him, I would *not* go to school. Didn't he wonder how I could be as soundly asleep as all that? That sick, we had better call an ambulance. Not a word was spoken. Kind man that he is, he let me sleep.

He walked out of the room with heavy steps. He was on his way to the Bronx, while I looked forward to a wonderful day of pleasure: reading, dreaming, listening to records, thinking, talking to my mother. I heard him plod down the steps. The front door slammed. The car started.

"You little shit," whispered a voice inside my head. *"He can take it. Why can't you?"*

ROBERT HAYDEN

THOSE WINTER SUNDAYS

Sundays too my father got up early
and put his clothes on in the blueblack cold,
then with cracked hands that ached
from labor in the weekday weather made
banked fires blaze. No one ever thanked him.

I'd wake and hear the cold splintering, breaking.
When the rooms were warm, he'd call
and slowly I would rise and dress,
fearing the chronic angers of that house,

Speaking indifferently to him,
who had driven out the cold
and polished my good shoes as well.
What did I know, what did I know
of love's austere and lonely offices?

NICHOLAS GAGE

. . . As I pushed open the screen door, the three people waiting in the kitchen turned to look at me: my sisters Glykeria and Olga at the kitchen table, and a uniformed policeman who was standing up, from my perspective appearing to be about eight feet tall.

My sisters, of course, got in the first word, shrieking in Greek like two banshees. "Accursed wretch, what have you brought down upon our heads?" they chorused.

The officer of the law took over, talking just like they did on *Dragnet*. "Are you Nicholas?"

"Yes," I answered meekly.

"Did you take your brother-in-law's car without permission earlier today?"

"Yes."

"Did you proceed to hit another car at the corner of Zenith Drive and May Street and then leave the scene of the accident?"

"Yes" (very quietly)

"Come with me, please. I'm going to have to take you down to headquarters and book you."

As if on cue, my father appeared at the back door, out of breath. He had been driving around Worcester, looking for me. His reaction to my crime was all I needed to make my day complete.

I turned to face the onslaught of his fury and stared: his face was wreathed in a beatific smile, which shone on me and the police officer alike. This did not reassure me, however, for I recognized the Mediterranean smile that masks emotions too terrible to be revealed. In *The Iliad* Homer described the fear that spread through the Trojan army when Ajax advanced "smiling under his threatening brows." Seeing my father, I knew exactly how the Trojans felt.

"I'm taking your son in to book him," the cop told my father.

"Is that really necessary, sir?" my father asked. "He's good boy—never make trouble. To be arrested, a criminal, spoil his good name . . ."

"I'll tell you what," the cop said in a milder tone. "It's time for my dinner break. If, while I was at dinner, you and your son should go to police headquarters and he turned himself in voluntarily, it would look a lot better later in court."

"You very kind man," Father said. "I don't forget this favor. Perhaps another favor, if I may ask. Do you know the name and number of the man in the other car? We must call him and apologize."

"All right," said the officer, pulling a piece of paper from his pocket. "But you didn't get this from me."

The policeman left and Father went to the phone and dialed Peter Bell, the diminutive lawyer whom all the Greeks turned to when they needed legal help. He arranged to meet Bell at the police station and then motioned me out the door as my sisters shouted advice after us.

I entered the green Plymouth feeling like a condemned man and waited for my father's wrath to fall, but he just drove in silence, staring straight ahead over the top of the steering wheel, deep in thought. Then he looked at me and that eerie smile reappeared on his face.

"Don't worry, my child, Peter Bell will fix everything.

He knows everyone in Worcester," he said. "It'll be all right. I'll call up the man in the other car and talk to him, make him understand. He probably has children himself. I'll talk to him man to man."

This was too strange for me to deal with. I decided he was just trying to reassure me so I would be calm at the police station, and I braced myself for the outburst that would come after I was booked.

In the station they booked me, took fingerprints, photographed me, then left us alone with our lawyer. Pete Bell shook my hand and greeted me like one recently bereaved, then began whispering to my father, who nodded sagely at everything he said.

Bell explained that if we could convince Dino to say there was a tacit understanding that I could use his car, then that part of my crime would become taking a car without permission instead of car theft—a misdemeanor instead of a felony.

"No problem at all," my father assured him. "Dino will say whatever I tell him to say."

I gathered that Dino had lost his famous temper when the police had arrived at Putnam and Thurston, demanding to see his car and then inviting him to the police station. Dino told them that unless they were prepared to pay his salary, he wasn't going anywhere. Finally the police appealed to Charley Davis, the owner of the restaurant, who said he would send Dino to the police after the rush hour. But as soon as Dino saw the damage to his car he had a pretty good idea who had caused it, and he told the police, who went to my house to wait for me.

After I was booked and became a sixteen-year-old with a criminal record, my father drove me home in the same unsettling silence that had so unnerved me on the way down. When we got in the door, he cut short the questions and condemnations of my sisters with a few terrifying roars of "Leave the boy alone!" Then we all sat at the dining room table near the cubbyhole that held the telephone, and listened as he dialed my accuser.

Ever since the accident, which seemed to have taken place in slow motion, my senses had been preternaturally sharp, and now I could clearly hear everything the man on the other end of the phone said, as well as my father's solemn voice.

"Mr. John, sir, I'm Christy Gage, Nick's father," he began. "I call to say we very, very sorry what happened. The boy panicked, made a big mistake. He's a good boy— never any trouble. Good student. Serious boy. Our lawyer say, if you don't press charges, it will save his life, not ruin his future and his good name."

"Are you out of your mind?" came the explosive voice on the other end, each word like the blow of a hammer. "Your boy left me on the street—I could have been bleeding to death! He might have killed me. He's a menace, and I'm going to do everything I can to see he's locked up for a goddamn long time."

My father's face suffused with color and the veneer of politeness crumbled. "What kind of man, you?" he shouted. "Want to ruin my boy's life. You must be sick person, to do that. He's only sixteen years old."

He slammed down the phone and turned to look at the rest of us with defeat in his eyes.

Instead of despair, I felt a surge of joy. This was the first time I had ever seen my father defend me. But then I realized that the words he had used were chosen to sway the man on the other end of the phone and influence him to go easy on our family's reputation.

A date was set for the arraignment and we all gathered in court: Peter Bell, my father, and me, feeling like a guest star in a "Perry Mason" episode. My father still hadn't punished me for my rampage of crime, and I was almost groggy from bracing myself for the first blow.

Peter Bell pleaded guilty on my behalf to taking a car without permission, reckless driving, and leaving the scene of an accident. Then he spoke in my defense: "Your Honor, this unhappy incident was the result of youthful immaturity, not malice. This young man panicked because of his inexperience. He arrived in this country a war refugee from Greece six years ago and has been a good boy until this tragedy: an altar boy, an excellent student, beyond reproach. He's never been in trouble before and comes from a very responsible family. His widowed father has been working in Worcester since 1910, struggling to support his family of five children, and is a model citizen. I ask you to take the boy's circumstances, his youth and good character into consideration."

The judge looked at me grimly. I was dressed in my Sunday blue suit and a tie and I hoped that my small stature and youthful appearance would sway him in my favor. "Is the boy's father here?" he asked, and my father stepped forward, clutching his hat, gazing in awe at the black-robed magistrate.

"I'm here, Judge," he said.

"Do you have anything to say about your son's actions before I pass sentence?" the judge asked.

"Mr. Judge, my boy is a good boy!" my father began. "He come from the worst of the civil war—nearly starve to death, escape with no shoes, guns and land mines everywhere, sent to refugee camp, lost his poor mother, murdered by Communist bastards. He come here to America, they put him in school with the dummies because he don't know the language. He have a hard time his first years, Mr. Judge. But this boy, he learn the English, he make fine grades, big success at school, work hard at the job, go to church at the altar every Sunday. It's my fault . . . I didn't get my childrens out in time to save my wife. My boy never know his father until late. I try, but I never was a father before. I know my boy, sir, and I know he don't mean to do bad things. He just forget what's right when he hit that car. But he's been through a lot and he's very, very sorry. Please forgive my son, Mr. Judge. I promise he will never do such a thing again. He's only learning about America now and this thing, if he go to jail, will ruin his life."

The judge was silent for several moments, thinking and studying me. I could see that my father's speech had moved him. As for me, I was shaken by Father's fervent defense of me. I had never known him to take my side before, and hearing him speak so emotionally about my problems when I had arrived surprised and touched me. Nevertheless, I still suspected that he was talking for the benefit of the court and in the end would show me the fury he really felt. I was so busy trying to figure him out that I hardly heard when the judge began to speak.

"Stand up, Nicholas," he said. "You know this is a very serious matter. What you did was not just a youthful indiscretion, it was a crime that could have led to serious injury, even death. Do you understand that?"

"Yes, sir."

"You must be made to accept your responsibility. When

you commit a crime in this country, you have to pay for it. No one else, including your father, can do it for you."

I didn't like the direction he was taking and frowned under his gaze as he went on.

"I will put you on probation," he said, "on the condition that you personally work to make full restitution for the damage to both cars, which, I am told, comes to $234 for the complainant's car and $120 for your brother-in-law's car. Your father is working hard to support you and your sisters and doesn't deserve this extra burden. He must promise me in writing that you will earn the money yourself and he won't give you any." He turned to my father. "Do I have your word on this, Mr. Christy?"

"Oh yes, Mr. Judge, sir," my father quickly replied.

"Then it is understood, Nicholas, that you will be on probation until all these moneys are paid and that your driver's license will be revoked for the duration. You will report weekly to a probation officer and the damages will be paid to the court as you earn them. Do you understand?"

"Yes, Your Honor," I muttered, as anger at the severity of my sentence rose in me.

Although Father and Peter Bell seemed relieved, I felt that I had been given a harsher sentence than I deserved. All the juvenile delinquents, arsonists, and petty thieves who had come up to the bench ahead of me had gotten away with just probation, but I had to work to pay expenses besides. By the time I was off probation and got my license back, I suspected, I'd be too old to drive *or* to seduce girls.

Nevertheless, Peter Bell was feeling very pleased with himself. My father, no doubt contemplating what he would have to pay Bell in fees, was less jubilant.

"The good thing," Bell told us, "is that Nick is a minor,

so his name won't appear in the papers, and once he completes his sentence the record will be expunged."

My father thanked him for what he had done, although I felt he deserved no congratulations. My depression increased when I headed for Father's Plymouth and braced myself for the retribution he had been saving up for so long. But in the car he only said to me, "I'm sorry I can't help you out with the money, but you heard what the judge said. I gave him my word I wouldn't."

"I'll earn it all," I said, spitting out each word. It seemed like a life sentence to me, but I was determined to do it.

At home, my oldest sisters, posed like the three Fates, were waiting to hear the sentence. When Father explained it to them, they all started shouting at once: it wasn't enough, it should have been worse . . . it was time to teach me a lesson . . . maybe if they locked me up, I'd grow into a decent man instead of a hoodlum who brings disgrace on his family.

"Let the boy alone—he's suffered enough!" roared my father, and I stared at him in astonishment. But nothing could stop my sisters once they became intoxicated by their own rhetoric, inspiring each other to greater and greater feats of condemnation. "It's impossible to plug them up!" Father explained to me in exasperation. "Come, Nikola. Let's get out of here."

He hurried out the door with me in his wake and my sisters screaming even louder at our backs. We got in his car and he began to drive while I stared at him in wonder. When I heard him defend me against my sisters, I understood for the first time that he was never going to unleash his anger on me.

EDWARD SEROTTA

When I was a teen-ager, I used to think my dad had been put on earth only to embarrass me. Now that I look back on it, I'm quite sure of it. I mean some guys' fathers were tyrannical, overachieving entrepreneurs who *made* their sons sell doughnuts at the corner every Sunday. Other guys I knew spent childhoods competing with goading ex-athletes, who derived joy from burning holes in their children with tennis balls blasted from the far court. Me? My dad had a single lifelong obsession, to be practical, to choose the pragmatic path. It was his religion. His *Bible* was *Consumer Reports*.

Even when I hear the word *practical* today (the dreaded P word, my sister calls it), my mind's eye races back to see a pint-size electric lawn mower, a storage freezer the size of a swimming pool, a used black-and-white TV built like some Mayan pyramid and, worst of all, the most hideous array of used cars ever seen outside the Iron Curtain.

Quick, how many kids do *you* know who were driven to school in a DKW? I don't even know what it was, but we sure had one—the only one, I think, in Chattanooga, Tennessee, in the mid-Sixties. A 1946 Dodge with something called Fluid-Drive (it took both hands to shift gears and improved my mother's bowling game immensely), and while it might have been quite the snappy set of wheels once, we had that sucker in 1965! A Studebaker so rickety and rust-eaten, not only would no one car-pool with us but also women would cross themselves as we drove by. All the kids in the neighborhood gathered around it on its fifteenth birthday, gave the poor thing a combination confirmation and bar mitzvah (who knew from a name like Studebaker —this was Tennessee, after all).

But these were things I could live with, because you could always *slump down* when you were riding around with your parents. But by my sixteenth birthday, Dad decided it was time to get a second car, one he and I, with my newly acquired license, could share. One night over banana milkshakes made in his trusty Oster ("This thing's been with your mother and me since our wedding. You'd be surprised how little maintenance it takes to . . ."), we struck a deal, man to man. If I would pick up repair jobs for his jewelry store and drop off a few collection letters ("They'll *never* hit a kid—I could probably lease you out to the optometrist down the street"), he would buy a brand-new ("Well, as new as you can get for six hundred dollars") set of wheels.

Together we searched the used-car lots of East Tennessee, they of the Flapping Triangular Flag, Sea of Naked Lightbulbs and ex-linebackers-named-Buck variety. I spent weeks grabbing the old man by his suspenders, keeping him from the ultra-bargains on the back row; the Henry Js, Crosleys and Hudson Hornets ("Of course, they don't make them anymore; that's why they're so cheap! Why you'd be surprised how little maintenance . . .").

One day I stumbled upon my dream car . . . a six-year-old absolute I-Swear-to-God cream puff Corvair Monza. White two-door little thing with those big oversized buckets inside (like movie-theater loveseats, really), and the only car in the world designed to look just like an electric shaver. It was $650, clean as a whistle, just what I needed to look cool for school. I dragged Dad along. "Hmm. I like the fact it's air-cooled. They can't charge you for that, can they?"

I dreamt of jealous eyes, and heavily lidded and lazily delivered lines like, "Hey, Wanda May, wanna get a chili dog and a cherry Coke in my new Corvair?" knowing she'd think I was hip.

Then, the bubble burst. One night Dad drove home wildly honking his way down the driveway ("No reason to buy up on a hill; all you get's a view. Down here, we get more house for less money") and in the glow of yellow buglights I found myself staring at a 1962 Rambler American 330 station wagon.

I tried to speak. "But . . . it's a wagon . . ."

"Think of all the deliveries you can make!" he chortled, thumping the hood. "And I got 'er from a schoolteacher."

"No doubt. And . . . it's so *green!*"

"Don't kid yourself. First thing that sold me on 'er. Safety! Stands out on a rainy day, right?"

"And, Dad, it's a *Rambler!*"

"And don't cha just know it! Take a look; fold-down seat converts to a bed! Kiss motels goodbye, son. Now isn't that the essence of *practical!*"

I staggered toward the house. A Rambler! Speak of the bubonic plague, zits on prom night, rattlesnakes in your bed—nothing was scarier to a teen-age boy posturing his way toward manhood than being seen in a *Rambler* (unless, of course, it was having that Lark Station Wagon with the sliding roof). Only guys who worked in the school library, those dweebs with the heavy keychains, the bad complexions and the Coke-bottle-thick glasses—they were the only ones who drove *Ramblers*.

I threw myself on the bed. It was September and school

was just starting. I thought of leaving home, joining the French Foreign Legion, changing my name. Then, a better idea seeped into my brain; I smiled and thought: Revenge!

On Judgment Day, if there is a war-crimes trial for teenagers who abused their parents' cars, I will spend several eternities in that big Spandau in the sky. I approached that poor car from Day One like a hungry lion sizing up a mess of Christians in the Roman Forum, or an actor trying out for a prison guard in *Midnight Express*. I mean I couldn't even wrap my fingers around its steering wheel without licking my lips with malicious glee, thinking of new and inventive forms of torture to administer.

Sitting at stoplights, I would slip the little nerdule into neutral and rev it up as high as it would go. Then calmly drop 'er into low. Buck! Bang! Shudder! The poor beast would fly off the ground like a Harrier jump jet zapped with a cattle prod, followed by a gagging fit before it managed to limp away. And brakes! Never touched 'em. I jammed those som 'bitches to the floor like I was squashing a fat, ugly spider; *every single time*. I found an old dirt road that had once been a railroad bed on the side of Lookout Mountain near the Georgia line and made suicide runs along its ruddy trail fast enough to fry the leaves on overhanging branches.

Yet jamming those gears hard enough to twist the driveshaft into a pretzel didn't faze her. Taking the oil out only made it run better. And there wasn't a single dirt road in all of East Tennessee that could shake her down. It was a contest, and before too long I realized something amazing. *I was losing*. That Rambler was The Thing That Wouldn't Die.

After a winter of carting busloads of kids and cargo

through town and my last high school summer by the lake (and, yes, that fold-down seat did come in handy), I made ready one September afternoon to head north to Knoxville, college and the Sixties that had already enveloped the rest of America. I loaded the Rambler, and with Dad beside me, we puttered off.

"It's a jungle out there, son," the old man told me, Laertes style. "Why, they've got department stores that prey on the gullible, restaurants that don't give you the price when you ask for 'Tonight's Special,' and gasoline that is far too overpriced." Nothing was just Overpriced to him, it was always Far Too. "Still and all, I hope I've set a good example for you, and I hope that you've seen that the Corvair would have been quite a foolish waste of money compared to our little Rambler, aye?"

I said nothing.

"Besides, what else could have stood up to the inhumane punishment you put this poor beast through? I'm figuring the way you treated this thing, you worked off a couple of decades of hostility."

I stared ahead in silence, feeling my face grow red, my eyes glued to the white lines zipping by the left front fender. I thought to myself: *The things our fathers know about us, all those deep secrets we feel are so safe—they are the ones they leave alone, to us and our adolescent madness.*

Finally I said, "Yeah, I guess so," and stole a glance in his direction. But he was busy figuring out mileage and not another word was said.

The round mellow hills rolled on before us. I guided the Rambler over lonely State Highway 58; somewhere that day, I left my childhood on the road behind me. I'm still not sure where.

IVAN DOIG

At dawn, the pewter sky beginning to warm to blue above the Castles across the valley, Dad and I already were stepping from the Jeep at timberline on Grass Mountain. Grandma had climbed out of bed when we did, given us coffee and sweet rolls, made sandwiches out of her thick crisp-crusted bread, saw us out the door with: *Don't bring home more grouse than all of Ringling can eat.* Beside her on the porch Spot stood planted in astonishment and alarm that he wasn't being invited into the Jeep with us. Dad hesitated: *No, fella. Not today.*

September frost underfoot, a testing frost, the lightest dust of white on the broad bunchgrass crest of mountain. Dad handed me the single-shot .22, then the small box of bullets to put in my jacket pocket. I shook out a cartridge, barely longer than my thumbnail, clicked it into the breech. Carrying the light rifle underhand on the side of my body away from Dad, I started along the mountain slope beside him.

He had a hunter's voice, which could soften just enough not to carry far and yet be heard clearly. My own nosedived in and out of mutter as I answered him. He showed me herding sites remembered from three decades before, game trails angling up and across the summit like age-lines on a vast forehead, homestead splotches on the saged skirts of the valley far below us. In trade, I told him everything I knew of my half-year ahead, basic training at the Air Force base in San Antonio, a technical school probably elsewhere in Texas for the rest of those months. The first grouse caught us both in midstep as it flailed like a hurled wad of gray leaves into the air in front of us.

That must've been one of yours, I said.

And who's carrying the gun along like a crowbar froze to his hand? As ready and free a laugh as I could ever remember from my father. *Ye could at least have throwed it at him.*

In minutes, I shot the next grouse before it could fly. I handed Dad the rifle: *Here, see if you learned anything from that.* I put the bird in the sack he held out to me, followed it seconds later with the one he shot from the top of a log fifty yards away. *I like to give mine a bit of a chance, ye see, instead of sneakin' up till I'm standin' on their tailfeathers.*

The rifle traded back and forth, we each missed shots, made more. At midmorning and four birds apiece, we knew the hunting was over, but kept walking the mountainside. *Right about over there, up over that little park ye see,* Dad pointed. *A time, there was a whole bunch, ten or twelve of us, ridin' back to the Basin from a dance at Deep Creek one night. Even Mrs. Christison, she was up in years, she was along with us. We got caught in a blizzard up here and all got lost off the road, the whole bunch of us goin' in a circle for about two hours. Finally we decided the best thing to do was just to sit down, wait and see if it'd clear up. We got off our horses—it wasn't cold; snowin' like sixty, but it was warm—and sat down on a bank there. After a while it let up and the moon come out so we could look around, and the whole damn lot of us were sittin' right square on the road.*

At early noon, we sat on a silvered log and ate our sandwiches dry.

Ye leave . . . when, day after tomorrow?

Yes.

Scared any of the plane ride?

Some. You know I'm like Grandma on that, leery about heights.

Unh-huh. His instant slant of grin. *As the fellow says, what if ye get up in that thing and it comes uncranked up there?*

Thanks a whole helluva lot for the idea.

I was up in one once, ye know. Nothin' to it.

Disbelief as if he'd said he'd once been to Afghanistan. *When the hell was that?*

When I was a punk kid about your age, at a rodeo or a fair or some kind of doin's. A guy had one of them planes with wings top and bottom, and he'd take ye up for a little ride. Angus and I bet each other five dollars about goin' up, and we're both so damn Scotch we didn't want to lose that money. I went first, I was the oldest. That guy turned that plane every which way, I'm here to tell ye. 'Well, how was it?' Angus says. 'If ye see my stomach up there,' I says, 'bring it back down with ye.'

You're a world of encouragement. I pitched a stone at a snag below us on the slope.

What about after this Air Force business? Are ye gonna be able to look for a job out here?

I faced around to him slowly, as if the motion hurt. *Dad, I don't think so. The jobs for me just aren't here. I think I'm pretty much gone from this country.*

I figured ye were. My father's straight, clean-lined face broke open in a tearful gulp, the wrenched gasp I had seen all the years ago in the weeks after my mother's death. I helplessly looked aside, swallowed, pulled at my lower lip with my teeth. . . .

MIKE HARDEN

My time came the year I turned sixteen. I was sitting at the dining room table when some flip comment brought a sharp right from my father, carrying with it the dare to finish the matter outside. It was his "pantywaist" taunt again, but it incited only pity from me. Anger he could deal with. At most it would cost him a tooth or two. But not pity.

That incident with my father changed us. He gave grudging acceptance to my coming of age. In return, I recited psalms to a god I no longer believed omnipotent. It was an uneasy peace. Even after I had graduated from high school and left home for the service, it was awkward for my father and me to absolve ourselves and each other of transgressions real and imagined. Still, etched clearly in my consciousness is the memory of an autumn afternoon in 1968 when we tried to make our peace.

We had gone hunting together. Had it been an earnest search for game, the afternoon would have been wasted. But in reality we were saying goodbye. I was leaving for Vietnam, and though terms of endearment from male to male came as hard to my family as ordering from a Portuguese menu, he was trying to say something.

We sat in a clearing deep in the woods at opposite ends of a fallen tree, cradling unfired rifles in our laps, watching dusk sponge the last light from the October sky. The tension was unbearable. I longed to see some movement, any movement, in the brush so I could raise my gun and break the silence. When it became too much, we rose, made our way back to the car and began the trip home.

Nothing was said until he turned onto the river road. Then, gripping the wheel, staring as though he were addressing not me but the bumper of the car ahead, he managed, "I want you to know I'm proud of you, always have been. If there was a way that I could take your place for you, you know I'd do it. I'll miss you. I'm not much good at it, but I'll try to write."

He did. His letter, soiled and dog-eared, is the only one I kept from that time.

I never understood how much he missed me until, many years later, a friend of his recalled an incident that occurred in a tavern while I was gone.

"Your old man was shooting pool," the friend remembered, "and some loudmouth farmer—big, strapping guy— was standing around talking about Vietnam. I could see it was bothering your dad, but he didn't say anything. Finally this guy, who had a boy about your age in college, said, 'Well, you've got to keep some of the smarter ones home so they can run this country.' He never knew what hit him. Your dad was across the pool table before I could grab him. He was only half this guy's size, but he had him pinned on his back on the shuffleboard machine with a pool cue across his throat, trying to choke him to death. It took four of us to pull your dad off of him.

PAUL HEMPHILL

Those were the days of unblinking idolatry: that glorious time of puberty when I tried to wear my cap like his, and affected his hillbilly twang, and wondered what it took to be able to smoke and chew a cigar at the same time, and marveled at his ability to back a heaving trailer into the tightest hole. On summer evenings, at dusk, there was the great excitement of stuffing fresh socks and underwear into a bag and waiting impatiently for him to announce it was time to be going. "Now, Paul, I don't want him growing up to be a truck driver," my mother would caution. "It's good enough for me," he would say, "and I notice you ain't starving."

And a large part of growing up would begin to take place as we hit the road, father and son, discovering the world and discovering each other together. Sleeping all day in the simmering Southern heat, and riding all night to the songs of the whistling tires and the all-night country radio stations ("Ol' Ernest Tubb sings like a bullfrog, don't he?"). Seeing the big tankers parked at the Mobile docks, the traffic in Atlanta, the tarpaper shacks in Mississippi, the cattle in Texas and the mist along the Blue Ridge. The truck stops at three o'clock in the morning, with bug-eyed truckers so high on Bennies they can't feed the pinball machines fast enough. "Your boy there looks just like you, Paul," and, in response, "Well, the kid can't help it." Donora, Pa., where Stan Musial was born. Nashville, where the Opry is. Pittsburgh, where the Pirates play.

Blowing past a Greyhound on a straightaway, walking

around a curve to see if the scales were still open, standing on the running board to relieve ourselves while crawling up the Smokies, the jouncing of the cab and the pinup overhead bringing a curious new sensation to the groin. The mysterious hand signals exchanged with passing truckers, the wrecks and near-wrecks, the Cardinals game from St. Louis broadcast by Harry Caray, the black laborers begging to help unload at the docks in New Orleans. "Naw, ain't got but a partial load o' tires on," to the I.C.C. Inspector, and, a quarter-mile down the road, grabbing another gear, "Them boys just don't take their work serious enough." We had that to hold us together, and baseball—more than once we stood through Sunday doubleheaders to watch the Birmingham Barons play, then rushed home to work on my fielding until dark. . . .

So why, I am asking myself now, of all the good times we had together, why should I remember a bad one? The details are fuzzy. I must have been eighteen or so. He came in off the road, but something was wrong. There was shouting. He talked about leaving out again right after supper. My mother found a pint of booze in his overnight bag and, with hell-fire finality, flushed the contents down the toilet. He left. She and my sister were hysterical. *It's the son's place to go find him and talk to him.*

Bewildered, I got into the car and raced into town, to the lot cluttered with tires and rusty engines and oil pans. I could see him sitting all alone in a dark corner of the cab, swigging from a pint, and when I pulled up and parked in the gravel beside the truck, we tried not to look at each other. Blue lights laid a scary blanket over the lot. There was the desperate, choking putt-putt-putt-putt of a refrigerated trailer somewhere, broken by the occasional wail of a far-off train whistle, and after an interminable pause I heard myself say, "They're crying."

A gurgle, a cough. "Thought I'd get started early."

"How come you did it?"

"I don't know what you mean."

"Made 'em cry."

"What'd you come down here for?"

"Mama said. I don't know."

"She shouldn't o' done that."

"Well, she told me."

He tilted back his head and began draining the bottle, his Adam's apple quivering and some of the whisky dribbling off to the side of his face, and his eyes looked like deep swollen ponds. I looked down and toed the gravel with my shoe while he finished. He sniffed and cleared his throat and then spoke in a frightened, vulnerable voice, a voice I had never heard come out of him before. "I'm not runnin' anywhere. There's a lot a boy don't know. I don't mean to make your mother cry, but sometimes a man's, a man's—." His voice had broken and when I dared look up at his face, bleached white by the pale lights on the lot, I saw that my old man, too, was crying. . . .

That night in the lot haunted me for a long time. It isn't easy to look on and see your father brought to his knees by mysterious devils. There was, indeed, "a lot a boy don't know." To this day—since it was a moment that embarrassed us both, we have never discussed it—I don't know who the devils were. That would have been around 1954, when he was forty-three: about the time the Teamsters were beginning to make it difficult for independent, freewheeling "lease operators" of his breed to make it; about the time more money was needed for us than ever before, my having attained college age; about the time a woman's natural instincts for "respectability" were causing my mother to hack away at such issues as church and example-setting and a nicer house in a subdivision and a more secure job like driving a bus.

But the larger point is that I had seen him running scared, and it brought to me the first vague stirrings that life was not going to be easy or even fun; that life could be a bitch not above kicking you in the groin if you so much as winked at her; that there would be some terrible scars before it was done; that one day there would be a young boy looking up to me, wanting answers, and about all I might be able to give him in the way of solid advice would be to suggest he go into a clinch when they started working on the head. Here we had been working on the theory that he was unbeaten and untied, the last of the indomitable heroes, and now I knew differently and he knew I knew differently. From there, we began.

4

Mixed Feelings

JOHN CHEEVER

REUNION

The last time I saw my father was in Grand Central Station. I was going from my grandmother's in the Adirondacks to a cottage on the Cape that my mother had rented, and I wrote my father that I would be in New York between trains for an hour and a half, and asked if we could have lunch together. His secretary wrote to say that he would meet me at the information booth at noon, and at twelve o'clock sharp I saw him coming through the crowd. He was a stranger to me—my mother divorced him three years ago and I hadn't been with him since—but as soon as I saw him I felt that he was my father, my flesh and blood, my future and my doom. I knew that when I was grown I would be something like him; I would have to plan my campaigns within his limitations. He was a big, good-looking man, and I was terribly happy to see him again. He struck me on the back and shook my hand. "Hi, Charlie," he said. "Hi, boy. I'd like to take you up to my club, but's in the Sixties, and if you have to catch an early train I guess we'd better get something to eat around here." He put his arm around me, and I smelled my father the way my mother sniffs a rose. It was a rich compound of whiskey, after-shave lotion, shoe polish, woolens, and the rankness of a mature male. I hoped that someone would see us together. I wished that we could be photographed. I wanted some record of our having been together.

We went out of the station and up a side street to a restaurant. It was still early, and the place was empty.

The bartender was quarreling with a delivery boy, and there was one very old waiter in a red coat down by the kitchen door. We sat down, and my father hailed the waiter in a loud voice. *"Kellner!"* he shouted. *"Garçon! Cameriere! You!"* His boisterousness in the empty restaurant seemed out of place. "Could we have a little service here!" he shouted. "Chop-chop." Then he clapped his hands. This caught the waiter's attention, and he shuffled over to our table.

"Were you clapping your hands at me?" he asked.

"Calm down, calm down, *sommelier,*" my father said. "If it isn't too much to ask of you—if it wouldn't be too much above and beyond the call of duty, we would like a couple of Beefeater Gibsons."

"I don't like to be clapped at," the waiter said.

"I should have brought my whistle," my father said. "I have a whistle that is audible only to the ears of old waiters. Now, take out your little pad and your little pencil and see if you can get this straight: two Beefeater Gibsons. Repeat after me: two Beefeater Gibsons."

"I think you'd better go somewhere else," the waiter said quietly.

"That," said my father, "is one of the most brilliant suggestions I have ever heard. Come on, Charlie, let's get the hell out of here."

I followed my father out of that restaurant into another. He was not so boisterous this time. Our drinks came, and he cross-questioned me about the baseball season. He then struck the edge of his empty glass with his knife and began shouting again. *"Garçon! Kellner! Cameriere! You!* Could we trouble you to bring us two more of the same."

"How old is the boy?" the waiter asked.

"That," my father said, "is none of your God-damned business."

"I'm sorry, sir," the waiter said, "but I won't serve the boy another drink."

"Well, I have some news for you," my father said. "I have some very interesting news for you. This doesn't happen to be the only restaurant in New York. They've opened another on the corner. Come on, Charlie."

He paid the bill, and I followed him out of that restaurant into another. Here the waiters wore pink jackets like hunting coats, and there was a lot of horse tack on the walls. We sat down, and my father began to shout again. "Master of the hounds! Tallyhoo and all that sort of thing. We'd like a little something in the way of a stirrup cup. Namely, two Bibson Geefeaters."

"Two Bibson Geefeaters?" the waiter asked, smiling.

"You know damned well what I want," my father said angrily. "I want two Beefeater Gibsons, and make it snappy. Things have changed in jolly old England. So my friend the duke tells me. Let's see what England can produce in the way of a cocktail."

"This isn't England," the waiter said.

"Don't argue with me," my father said. "Just do as you're told."

"I just thought you might like to know where you are," the waiter said.

"If there is one thing I cannot tolerate," my father said, "it is an impudent domestic. Come on, Charlie."

The fourth place we went to was Italian. *"Buon giorno,"* my father said. *"Per favore, possiamo avere due cocktail americani, forti, forti. Molto gin, poco vermut."*

"I don't understand Italian," the waiter said.

"Oh, come off it," my father said. "You understand Italian, and you know damned well you do. *Vogliamo due cocktail americani. Subito.*"

The waiter left us and spoke with the captain, who came over to our table and said, "I'm sorry, sir, but this table is reserved."

"All right," my father said. "Get us another table."

"All the tables are reserved," the captain said.

"I get it," my father said. "You don't desire our patronage. Is that it? Well, the hell with you. *Vada all' inferno.* Let's go, Charlie."

"I have to get my train," I said.

"I'm sorry, sonny," my father said. "I'm terribly sorry." He put his arm around me and pressed me against him. "I'll walk you back to the station. If there had only been time to go up to my club."

"That's all right, Daddy," I said.

"I'll get you a paper," he said. "I'll get you a paper to read on the train."

Then he went up to a newsstand and said, "Kind sir, will you be good enough to favor me with one of your Goddamned, no-good, ten-cent afternoon papers?" The clerk turned away from him and stared at a magazine cover. "Is it asking too much, kind sir," my father said, "is it asking too much for you to sell me one of your disgusting specimens of yellow journalism?"

"I have to go, Daddy," I said. "It's late."

"Now, just wait a second, sonny," he said. "Just wait a second. I want to get a rise out of this chap."

"Goodbye, Daddy," I said, and I went down the stairs and got my train, and that was the last time I saw my father.

ALFRED LUBRANO

My father and I were college buddies back in the mid-1970s. While I was in class at Columbia, struggling with the esoterica du jour, he was on a bricklayer's scaffold not far up the street, working on a campus building.

Sometimes we'd hook up on the subway going home, he with his tools, I with my books. We didn't chat much about what went on during the day. My father wasn't interested in Dante, I wasn't up on arches. We'd share a *New York Post* and talk about the Mets.

My dad has built lots of places in New York City he can't get into: colleges, condos, office towers. He makes his living on the outside. Once the walls are up, a place takes on a different feel for him, as if he's not welcome anymore. It doesn't bother him, though. For my father, earning the dough that paid for my entrée into a fancy, bricked-in institution was satisfaction enough, a vicarious access.

We didn't know it then, but those days were the start of a branching off, a redefining of what it means to be a workingman in our family. Related by blood, we're separated by class, my father and I. Being the white-collar son of a blue-collar man means being the hinge on the door between two ways of life. . . .

. . . My father has had a tough time accepting my decision to become a mere newspaper reporter, a field that pays just a little more than construction does. He wonders why I haven't cashed in on that multi-brick education and taken on some lawyer-lucrative job. After bricklaying for thirty years, my father promised himself I'd never pile bricks and blocks into walls for a living. He figured an education—genielike and benevolent—would somehow rocket me into the consecrated trajectory of the upwardly mobile, and load some serious loot into my pockets. What he didn't count on was his eldest son breaking blue-collar rule No. 1: Make as much money as you can, to pay for as good a life as you can get.

He'd tell me about it when I was nineteen, my collar already fading to white. I was the college boy who handed him the wrong wrench on help-around-the-house Saturdays. "You better make a lot of money," my blue-collar handy dad wryly warned me as we huddled in front of a disassembled dishwasher I had neither the inclination nor the aptitude to fix. "You're gonna need to hire someone to hammer a nail into a wall for you."

In 1980, after college and graduate school, I was offered my first job, on a now-dead daily paper in Columbus, Ohio. I broke the news in the kitchen, where all the family business is discussed. My mother wept as if it were Vietnam. My father had a few questions: "Ohio? Where the hell is Ohio?"

I said it's somewhere west of New York City, that it was like Pennsylvania, only more so. I told him I wanted to write, and these were the only people who'd take me.

"Why can't you get a good job that pays something, like in advertising in the city, and write on the side?"

"Advertising is lying," I said, smug and sanctimonious, ever the unctuous undergraduate. "I wanna tell the truth."

"The truth?" the old man exploded, his face reddening as it does when he's up twenty stories in high wind. "What's truth?" I said it's real life, and writing about it would make me happy. "You're happy with your family," my father said, spilling blue-collar rule No. 2. "That's what makes you happy. After that, it all comes down to dollars and cents. What gives you comfort besides your family? Money, only money."

During the two weeks before I moved, he reminded me that newspaper journalism is a dying field, and I could do better. Then he pressed advertising again, though neither of us knew anything about it, except that you could work in Manhattan, the borough with the water-beading high gloss, the island polished clean by money. I couldn't explain myself, so I packed, unpopular and confused. No longer was I the good son who studied hard and fumbled endearingly with tools. I was hacking people off.

One night, though, my father brought home some heavy tape and that clear, plastic bubble stuff you pack your mother's second-string dishes in. "You probably couldn't do this right," my father said to me before he sealed the boxes and helped me take them to UPS. "This is what he wants," my father told my mother the day I left for Columbus in my grandfather's eleven-year-old gray Cadillac. "What are you gonna do?" After I said my good-byes, my father took me aside and pressed five one-hundred-dollar bills into my hands. "It's okay," he said over my weak protests. "Don't tell your mother."

When I broke the news about what the paper was paying me, my father suggested I get a part-time job to augment the income. "Maybe you could drive a cab." Once, after I was chewed out by the city editor for something trivial, I made the mistake of telling my father during a visit home. "They pay you nothin', and they push you around too much in that business," he told me, the rage building. "Next time, you gotta grab the guy by the throat and tell him he's a big jerk."

"Dad, I can't talk to the boss like that."

"Tell him. You get results that way. Never take any shit." A few years before, a guy didn't like the retaining wall my father and his partner had built. They tore it down and did it again, but the guy still bitched. My father's partner shoved the guy into the freshly laid bricks. "Pay me off," my father said, and he and his partner took the money and walked. Blue-collar guys have no patience for office politics and corporate bile-swallowing. Just pay me off and I'm gone. Eventually, I moved on to a job in Cleveland, on a paper my father has heard of. I think he looks on it as a sign of progress, because he hasn't mentioned advertising for a while.

When he was my age, my father was already dug in with a trade, a wife, two sons and a house in a neighborhood in Brooklyn not far from where he was born. His workaday, family-centered life has been very much in step with his immigrant father's. I . . . idealized my dad as a kind of dawn-rising priest of labor, engaged in holy ritual. Up at five every day, my father has made a religion of responsibility. My younger brother, Chris, a Wall Street white-collar guy with the sense to make a decent salary, says he always felt safe when he heard Dad stir before him, as if Pop were taming the day for us. My father, fifty-five years old, but expected to put out as if he were three decades stronger, slips on machine-washable vestments of khaki cotton without waking my mother. He goes into the kitchen and turns on the radio to catch the temperature. Bricklayers have an occupational need to know the weather. And because I am my father's son, I can recite the five-day forecast at any given moment.

My father isn't crazy about this life. He wanted to be a singer and actor when he was young, but that was frivolous doodling to his Italian family, who expected money to be coming in, stoking the stove that kept hearth fires ablaze. Dreams simply were not energy-efficient. My dad learned a trade, as he was supposed to, and settled into a life of pre-scripted routing. He says he can't find the black-and-white publicity glossies he once had made.

. . . My dad wanted a civil-service, bricklayer foreman's job that wouldn't be so physically demanding. There was a written test that included essay questions about construction work. My father hadn't done anything like it in forty years. Why the hell they needed bricklayers to write essays I have no idea, but my father sweated it out. Every morning before sunrise, Chris would be ironing a shirt, bleary-eyed, and my father would sit at the kitchen table and read aloud his practice essays on how to wash down a wall, or how to build a tricky corner. Chris would suggest words and approaches.

It was so hard for my dad. He had to take a Stanley Kaplan–like prep course in a junior high school three nights a week after work for six weeks. At class time, the outside men would come in, twenty-five construction workers squeezing themselves into little desks. Tough blue-collar guys armed with No. 2 pencils leaning over and scratching out their practice essays, cement in their hair, tar on their pants, their work boots too big and clumsy to fit under the desks.

"Is this what finals felt like?" my father would ask me on the phone when I pitched in to help long-distance. "Were you always this nervous?" I told him yes. I told him writing's always difficult. He thanked Chris and me for the coaching, for putting him through school this time. My father thinks he did okay, but he's still awaiting the test results. In the meantime, he takes life the blue-collar way, one brick at a time.

When we see each other these days, my father still asks how the money is. Sometimes he reads my stories; usually he likes them, although he recently criticized one piece as being a bit sentimental: "Too schmaltzy," he said. . . .

During one of my visits to Brooklyn not long ago, he and I were in the car, on our way to buy toiletries, one of my father's weekly routines. "You know, you're not as successful as you could be," he began, blue-collar blunt as usual. "You paid your dues in school. You deserve better restaurants, better clothes." Here we go, I thought, the same old stuff. I'm sure every family has five or six similar big issues that are replayed like well-worn videotapes. I wanted to fast-forward this thing when we stopped at a red light.

Just then my father turned to me, solemn and intense. His knees were aching and his back muscles were throbbing in clockable intervals that registered in his eyes. It was the end of a week of lifting fifty-pound blocks. "I envy you," he said quietly. "For a man to do something he likes and get paid for it—that's fantastic." He smiled at me before the light changed, and we drove on. To thank him for the understanding, I sprang for the deodorant and shampoo. For once, my father let me pay.

ANTHONY WALTON

"*You can get by, but you can't get away.*" I kept hearing my father's voice, and it was annoying. Here I was, spending a beautiful Saturday morning in a Santa Monica hardware store instead of driving up the California coast or sleeping in.

I was sorting through aisles of plastic pipe connectors, all because someone had tried to get away with building a sprinkler system on the cheap. The system had ruptured, flooding my friend's yard and sidewalk. To avoid a hefty plumber's fee, we had to do the repairs ourselves. I couldn't help hearing my father again: "*Do it right the first time.*"

I've grown accustomed to hearing Claude's voice. As I've gotten older, I hear him almost every day, "*You're penny-wise and dollar-foolish.*" "*You got champagne tastes, but a water pocket.*" "*Don't believe everything you hear.*" As my friends and I run into brick walls working our way into adulthood, I am increasingly amazed at the sometimes brutal truth that my father has imparted in his seemingly offhand way.

One Christmas Eve, he and I were working on the furnace of a rental house he owns. It was about twenty below outside and, I thought, colder inside. Tormented by visions of a family-room fire, cocoa and pampering by my mother (I was home from college), I wanted my father to call it a day and get on with the festivities. After all, it *was* Christmas.

"We can't," said my father. "This is these people's

home. They should be home on Christmas." He continued wrenching and whanging on a pipe.

I saw an opening. "Exactly. *We* should be home on Christmas."

He shook his head. "It ain't that simple."

"It'd be simple to call somebody."

"You got a thousand dollars?"

"No. But you do."

"The reason I got it is, I don't give it away on things I can do myself."

A couple of hours later, when we had finished and were loading our tools into the car, he looked at me. "See? That wasn't so hard. But nobody can tell you nothing. That thousand dollars will come in handy. In fact, I'll probably have to send it to *you*." He shook his head, closed the trunk and said, "Boy, just keep on living."

"Just keep on living." I often thought it sounded like a threat, but now I see that he was challenging me to see the world as it is and to live in it responsibly. I was like a lot of kids I knew, middle-class, happy, successful at most of what I attempted—but largely at the expense (literally) of my father and the world he created. Now as I contemplate creating a world for his grandchildren, I gain more respect for such an accomplishment and the unblinking steadiness it takes.

My father is the kind of man overlooked or ridiculed by the media. His values—fidelity, simplicity and frugality—are spurned by younger people, but I am beginning to see that these are the very values that keep a society functioning.

"Boy, you got to get a routine." He has gone to a job he does not like, in a steel factory, for thirty-six years. One

day I asked him why, and he looked at me as if I had rocks in my head: "That's where the money is." And he has been married to the same woman for thirty-one years. "Marriage gives you a reason to do things."

As I gain more experience in a world where, it seems, virtually everything is disposable, I begin to appreciate the unsurpassed values of steadiness and limited objectives. I'm reminded of the television comedy "All in the Family," and how much of the humor was directed at the willfully uninformed, purposely contrary Archie Bunker. It occurs to me, as I contemplate buying my first house, that everyone else, including his son-in-law, Meathead, who gloried in putting Archie down, was sleeping in Archie's house and eating Archie's grub. I'm increasingly aware of how much security my father has brought to my adventures.

They were adventures he rarely understood. My father was born into excruciating poverty in rural Mississippi during the Depression. He had very little formal education, leaving school early to support his brothers and sisters, and bounced from Holly Springs, Miss., to Memphis to Chicago to the Air Force. But along the way he acquired a world view as logical as Newton's.

The first and most important law of the world according to Claude is *"Have the facts."* God is the only thing he takes on faith. Recently, searching for a new lawn tractor, he went to three different dealers and got three different prices for the same machine. *"I'm from just outside Missouri; you got to show me."* He then went to a fourth dealer and purchased a larger tractor for less money.

I used to laugh at one of his hobbies, analyzing financial tables. He would look up from half an hour of calculating and announce: "Did you know if you put five cents in the bank when Columbus came to America, at 5¼ interest compounded daily, today you'd have $1,000,565,162 (or some such figure)?" Now I phone him for advice about financing a house or a car, and I'm beginning to understand how he can own real estate and several cars, educate his kids and regularly bail those kids out of jams. *"Boy, a nickel only goes so many ways. But nobody can tell you nothing. Just keep on living."*

And I've kept on living, and surrendered a lot of illusions, one by one. Claude says, *"You reap what you sow."* I call this idea karma, that what goes around comes around. Claude cautioned me one night as I went out to break off with a girlfriend, "Remember, you got a sister." The notion that there was a link between my behavior and how I could expect my sister to be treated has served as a painfully clear guide ever since. And, in the current romantic and sexual climate, I like to think it's saved me some trouble. *"You can get by, but you can't get away."*

Claude values experience. I remember going with him in search of a family attorney. He decided against several without saying why, before suddenly settling on a firm right there in the office. On the way home he explained: "I was looking for a 'Daddy' kind of man. Somebody who's been through some battles, who's raised children. He had those pictures up of his grandchildren. That tells me what he values. And I think he's already made most of his mistakes." When I asked him where he had acquired all this insight he laughed. "I didn't get to be fifty and black by being stupid. You go around enough times, you begin to catch on."

Claude doesn't put a lot of stock in what he calls book learning. He says, "College never made anybody smart."

But he has financed about $100,000 worth of book learning —and endured its being thrown in his face until the thrower had to return, hat in hand, for one kind of aid or another.

This leads to another basic law: *"Be realistic."* Claude sees the world very clearly, and what he sees is often not pretty. "It was like this when I got here, and it's going to be like this when I leave, so I'm not going to worry about it." I'm coming to see the wisdom in this. Young people often have to experience the world for many years before they have a hint of understanding human nature and, more important, history. For this reason, they often misread the world. They do not understand that poverty, war and racism have always been conditions of human life. Worse, when confronted by the unrelenting intractability of these problems, they often abandon smaller, but equally worthy, goals.

Claude likes to say, *"If everybody would clean up his yard, the rest of the world would take care of itself."* That statement verges on oversimplification, but as a way of recognizing one's true responsibilities in the world it makes irreproachable sense.

This is probably the key to the world according to Claude—the power of limited objectives. By being realistic about our goals, we increase our chances of success in the long run. "Anything we do is going to be hard, and if it isn't hard, it's going to be difficult. But that just means it's going to take us a little longer." To me, this acceptance of the world and life as they are, and not as we would have them be, is the key to becoming an adult.

And so I am forced to acknowledge that the world according to Claude is increasingly, in my experience, the world as it is. I realize you *can't* put a price on a clear conscience, as Claude loves to say; very often the ability to live with one's self is all one can hope for. I'm beginning to see the power in, to spin a metaphor, not needing to play every single golf course on the planet; Claude has built a putting green in his back yard and mastered that. He has made his peace with the world, and that is enough.

Most of all, I realize that every time Claude said, *"Nobody can tell you nothing,"* he went ahead and told me something—and it was always the truth. Except maybe once. We were arguing, and I took exception to what I perceived as high-handedness. "You should respect me," I said. "We're supposed to be friends."

He looked at me gravely. "We are not *friends*. I am your father."

I haven't quite figured this out, because he is far from being my best friend. Sometimes I'm not sure we even know each other. But it seems he is the truest friend I have had, and can expect to have.

STANLEY ELKIN

... The forties were my father's decade. He looked like a man of the forties. The shaped fedora and the fresh haircut and the shined shoes. He was handsome, I mean. Like an actor in a diplomat's part, a star-crossed Secretary of State, say. Phil *looked* romantic. The noblesse oblige of his smile and the faint melodrama of the poses he struck in mirrors. His soft silver hair, gray since his 20s, the dark, carefully trimmed mustache, the widow's peak, the long patrician features, his good cheekbones like drawn swords. The vague rakishness of his face like a kind of wink. He was a traveling salesman, a rhinestone merchant, purveyor of costume jewelry to the trade. He worked in the Chicago offices of the old Great Northern Building at State and Jackson for Coro, Inc., which, in its time, was the largest manufacturer of "junk" jewelry in the world, and his territory was, well, immense, most of the Midwest—Wisconsin, Iowa, Minnesota, the Dakotas, Michigan but not Detroit, Illinois but not Chicago, Indiana but not Indianapolis, Missouri but not Kansas City or St. Louis. Some odd lot, under three flags arrangement of compromised spoils he had with Coro's New York headquarters like the divvy of armies of occupation. It was big enough, at any rate, to keep him on the road two months out of three— though he often managed to get home weekends—and when one heart attack too many forced him to slow down in the fifties, he had to hire three men to cover the ground for him while he stayed in the Great Northern in Chicago and worked the phones.

Calling the buyers, calling them darling, calling them sweetheart, calling them dear. And how much was *shmooz* and how much traveling salesman's protocol and how much true romance I really can't say. Though some was. Some must have been, I think. He must have been irresistible to those Minnesota and Indiana ladies. Wisconsin farmers' daughters, the girls of the Dakotas, the Michigan peninsular. Though maybe not. He didn't frequent bars; would have looked, and felt, out of place in the rough taverns where farmers and fishermen and hunters traded the time of day and did the shoptalk of field and stream, the gauge of a shotgun shell the test of a line. Would have hesitated to ask for rye, his drink and bread of choice. So not only can I not really say, I don't really know. He was no Willy Loman. I never asked him, "What happened in Philly, Philly?"

Nor would those farmers have understood *his* shoptalk— the spring and fall seasons something different to them than they were to him. Nor understood his enthusiasm for costume jewelry, interesting to him as treasure chest, pieces of eight—the paste pearl and glass gem, all the colored chips and beads of his trade, amorphous as platelets seen under a microscope, all the crystalline shards of the blood's streaming what the kaleidoscope saw, the bright complicated jigsaw of the toy realities, random and patchwork as a quilt.

Proud of how much money he earned, proud of his wit, his Hester Street smarts.

The price of admission to the movies when my father

was a kid was three cents, two for a nickel. He would range up and down the line calling, "I've got two cents; who's got three? I've got two; who's got three?"

Here are more traveling salesman stories.

When he first went on the road for Coro at the beginning of the Depression, my father worked out of New York City on a $35-a-week draw against commission, was given the clapboard and red-brick small towns of upstate New York for his territory. One day Mr. Rosenberger, the firm's president, called him into his office and told him that he was into the company for $200 or $300.

"I know," said my father.

"You know?"

"Sure," my father said. "This time next month it'll be another fifty dollars. In two months maybe another hundred more. In three more months it could be double what I owe you now. If I don't quit or you don't fire me, sooner or later I could bankrupt this company."

"Maybe I'd better fire you, then."

"Sure," my father said, "or give me a territory that isn't played out. Where the stores aren't all boarded up and the town's leading industry ain't torn shoelaces or selling apples by the bite."

It's the language of myth and risk and men sizing each other up. It's steely-eyed appraisal talk, I-like-the-cut-of-your-jib speech, and maybe that's not the way it happened. But that was the way my father told it and it became The Story of How They Gave Him the Central Standard Time Zone—"I've got two; who's got three? I've got two; who's got three?"—of how he moved west and took up his manifest destiny in the Chicago office.

This was the thirties and the beginning of my father's itinerancy on the road—it's the American metaphor—to his luck. (Automobiles he used, berths, compartments on trains, and once, during the war, he rode back to Chicago from Minneapolis in a caboose, and was possibly one of the first salesmen to use airplanes regularly. There were, I recall, preferred-customer cards from airlines in his wallets—and recall the wallets, too, their fat leather smoothed to use, all his leathers, his luggage and dop kits.) Some golden age of the personal we shared through his stories, his actor's resonances, all those anecdotes of self-dramatizing exigency, of strut and shuffle and leap and roll. In those days it was his America. . . .

We closed our apartment in the summers and went east, and one time—this would have been the forties, the last year of the war—I was staying over in Manhattan with my dad. (Though we had a place in Jersey, my father came out only on weekends and spent the rest of the week in one of the hotels around Herald Square near Coro's New York office—the Pennsylvania, the McAlpin, the Vanderbilt.) And this particular morning he was running late and said we would grab a quick breakfast at the Automat.

I was following him in the cafeteria line and the girl behind the counter asked what he wanted.

"Scrambled eggs," he said. "And some bacon."

"Bacon is extra," she said.

I thought he was going to hit her. He slammed his tray down and started to yell, to call her names.

"Goddamn you!" he shouted. "You stupid ass! Did I *ask* if bacon was extra? Do I *look* as if I can't afford extra goddamn bacon? *Who in the hell do you think you are?*"

"Take it easy, mister," said someone behind us in

line. "What do you want from her? She didn't mean anything."

"You shut up," my father warned him, "you shut up and mind your goddamn business!"

And the fellow did, terrified of the crazy man ahead of him in line. Then my father shoved some bills onto the counter and pulled me away.

I want to be careful here. What he did was terrible. He was something of a snob who didn't much care for what he would never have called "the element," but who may have thought like that, who had by heart in his head some personalized complex periodic table of the four-flusher fraudulent. (The element, yes, who traded in pseudo elements, in fractions and grosses of the manqué, the plated silver and the short karat.) But that woman had hit him where he lived, had touched some still-raw, up-from-Hester Street vulnerability he must have favored like a game leg. It was awful to see, but today I am sorrier for my father than I am for the woman. He *hated* four-flushers—it was the worst thing he could call you—and the thought that that woman behind the counter suspected something like that in him drove him, I think, temporarily insane. If they'd understood, no jury in the world would even have been *permitted* to convict him.

The other side of the coin is braver, his intact I've-got-two-who's-got-three instincts.

It was probably one of his milder heart attacks. He was to be discharged from the hospital that morning and my mother drove down from the North Side to fetch him home.

"How are you feeling?" his doctor asked.

"Not bad. A little shaky. Pretty good."

"You'll have to take it easy for a few weeks."

"Sure."

"Even after you go back to work I don't think you should drive for a while."

"Hey," my father said, "I know the drill."

When my mother brought the car around from the hospital lot he asked for the keys.

"Phil," said my mother, "you heard what he said."

"Come on, Tootsie. Give me the keys."

"But you're not supp—"

"Tootsie," he said, "give me the damn car keys."

The drive on the Outer Drive from the South to the North Side was practically a straight shot. There was this one stoplight, on Oak Street, in the few-hundred-north block. My father was a good driver but he looked at you when he spoke and was as much the raconteur in a moving automobile as in a living room. He could turn anything into an anecdote and he delighted in the voices, in the gestures. He was telling my mother a story and waving his arm about.

"Phil," she screamed, "the light!"

"What? Oh," he said, "yeah."

He continued to tell his story while waiting for the long light to change on Oak Street. Oldsmobiles in neutral have a tendency to creep. The impact wasn't great but it infuriated the other driver. He came pouring out of his car like a dirge, like a requiem mass, a big, beefy six-footer. He pulled the car door open on the driver's side and started to curse my father, who simply reached his hand into the inside pocket of his suit coat and held it there around an imaginary gun. He interrupted the big man's angry obscenities.

"Get back in your car," my father told him quietly. "I'm

counting to five. I'm not even bothering to count out loud."

The man held his arms up and backed off. Back in his car he ran the light. When it turned green again my father drove home.

When I was either seven or eight I bought my father a plaster-of-paris reproduction of the Statue of Liberty. It was more than a foot high and the torch was really a cigarette lighter. He took it out of the paper cone in which it had been wrapped like a rose and wanted to know where the hell I'd gotten such crap.

People, tender of the kiddy sensibilities, are appalled by his callousness and profess not to believe me when I tell them that I was grateful, at least after thinking it over. It was educational, a lesson in taste. I buy neither souvenirs nor novelty items. No pillows with ATLANTIC CITY embroidered in satin have ever graced my sofas. No miniature outhouses are as frontlets between my eyes, nor is there anything like them on the lintels of my house or on my gates. . . .

. . . Often, when my father went to New York, he would visit his sister Jean. One night when my cousin Bert came back from law school my father was in my aunt's apartment. She'd given him some supper and he'd gone to the sofa to lie down. He was moaning and Jean asked if he was uncomfortable, if there was anything she could do. (It was the 1950s now, the decade of his heart attacks, four in seven years, and he would wake up coughing in the middle of the night, hawking, hacking, trying with those terrible percussives to bring up the poisons from his flooded chest; it was the fifties now, the decade of his pain and death.)

"You work too hard, Phil. You'll kill yourself, working so hard. Slow down; take it easy. So you make a little less money. Your health is what matters."

My father said something she couldn't understand, and she leaned down to understand him better. "What, Phil? What's that?"

"My health," he said scornfully, louder now, and Bert could hear him, too. "Listen," he said, "if I have to live on ten thousand a year like some ribbon clerk I don't *want* to live."

So, maybe, in the long run, it ain't more blessed to give than receive; maybe picking up checks all 'round is not only hazardous to your health but disastrous to your character. But maybe he knew that and picked up the checks anyway, who behind his glass-jaw sensibilities only wanted another shot at that line, to be on it again, the roles reversed this time, what he really wanted only to call, *"I've* got three! *I've* got three; who's got two?"

EDWARD FIELD

A BILL TO MY FATHER

I am typing up bills for a firm to be sent to their clients.
It occurs to me that firms are sending bills to my father
Who has that way an identity I do not often realize.
He is a person who buys, owes, and pays,
Not papa like he is to me.
His creditors reproach him for not paying on time
With a bill marked "Please Remit."
I reproach him for never having shown his love for me
But only his disapproval.
He has a debt to me too
Although I have long since ceased asking him to come
across;
He does not know how and so I do without it.
But in this impersonal world of business
He can be communicated with:
With absolute assurance of being paid
The boss writes "Send me my money"
And my father sends it.

BOB GREENE

The event was a retirement dinner for a man who had spent forty years with the same company. A private dining room had been rented for the evening, and the man's colleagues from his office were in attendance. Speeches and toasts were planned, and a gift was to be presented. It was probably like a thousand other retirement dinners that were being held around the country that night, but this one felt a little different because the man who was retiring was my father.

I flew in for the dinner, but I was really not a part of it; a man's work is quite separate from his family, and the people in the room were as foreign to me as I was to them. To me most of them were names, overheard at the dinner table all my life as my father sat down to his meal after a day at the office; to them I was the kid in the framed photograph on my father's desk.

Names from a lifetime at the same job; it occurred to me, looking at the men and women in the room, that my father had worked for that same company since the time that Franklin Delano Roosevelt was president. Now my father was sixty-five, and the rules said that he must retire; looking at the faces of the men and women, I tried to recall the images of each of them that I had built up over the years at our family dinners.

My father was seated at a different table from me on this night; he appeared to be vaguely uncomfortable, and I could understand why. My mother was in the room, and my sister and brother; it was virtually the first time in my father's life that there had been any mix at all between his family and his work. The people at his office knew he had a family, and we at home knew he had a job, but that is as close as it ever came. And now we were all together. . . .

The speeches began, and, as I had expected, much of their content meant nothing to me. They were filled with references and in-jokes about things with which I was not familiar; I saw my father laughing and nodding his head in recognition as every speaker took his turn, and often the people in the room would roar with glee at something that drew a complete blank with me. And again it occurred to me: a man spends a life with you, but it is really only half a life; the other half belongs to a world you know nothing about.

The speeches were specific and not general; the men and women spoke of little matters that had happened over the course of the years, and each remembrance was like a small gift to my father, sitting and listening. None of us really changes the world in our lifetimes, but we touch the people around us in ways that may last, and that is the real purpose of a retirement dinner like this one—to tell a man that those memories will remain, even though the rules say that he has to go away.

I found myself thinking about that—about how my father was going to feel the next morning, knowing that for the first time in his adult life he would not be driving to the building where the rest of these people would be reporting for work. The separation pains have to be just as strong as to the loss of a family member, and yet in the world of the American work force, a man is supposed to accept it and even embrace it. I tried not to think about it too hard.

When it was my father's turn to speak, his tone of voice had a different sound to me than the one I knew from around the house of my growing up; at first I thought that it came from the emotion of the evening, but then it struck me that this probably was not true; the voice I was hearing probably was the one he always used at the office, the one I had never heard.

During my father's speech a waiter came into the room with a message for another man from the company; the man went to a phone just outside the room. From my table, I could hear him talking. There was a problem at the plant, something about a malfunction in some water pipes. The man gave some hurried instructions into the phone, saying which levers to shut off and which plumbing company to call for night emergency service.

It was a call my father might have had to deal with on other nights, but on this night the unspoken rule was that he was no longer part of all that. The man put down the phone and came back into the dining room, and my father was still standing up, talking about things unfamiliar to me.

I thought about how little I really know about him. And I realized that it was not just me; we are a whole nation of sons who think they know their father, but who come to understand on a night like this that they are really only half of their fathers' lives. Work is a mysterious thing; many of us claim to hate it, but it takes a grip on us that is so fierce that it captures emotions and loyalties we never knew were there. The gift was presented, and then, his forty years of work at an end, my father went back to his home, and I went back to mine.

STEVE MARCUS

Before a crippling stroke in 1972, my father was a man of business, the delicatessen business. After working for people for most of his life, he finally got his own business. Sam's Kosher Delicatessen and Restaurant was an elegant name for a ramshackle store in a decaying neighborhood of Bayside. My father fancied himself a restaurateur, but without the trappings. His restaurant consisted of six old dinette tables, a forever broken walk-in refrigerator and a toilet that did not flush. The store had no heat in the winter, no air-conditioning in the summer. Those who complained were told a repairman was on the way, though none had been called.

City inspectors who cited him for fire hazards in the kitchen were bribed with a few bucks and a few frankfurters. If his terms were not accepted, he would call them "Hitlers" and chase them from the store with a large butcher knife. It wasn't much of a place, but for sixteen hours a day, for twelve years, it was my father's place of business.

He had an extensive menu, left over from the former occupant, but my father penciled the words "chef is sick" across the inside of each one. There was no chef, save for my father, who would cook a roast beef he bought from Bohack's supermarket. He stuck a "strictly kosher" tag on the meat in fear a rabbi would come in to check. . . .

My brother and I went to work with my father on alternate weekends. He didn't let us do anything because in his estimation it wouldn't have been done correctly. So we would sit at a back table most of the day, waiting for our lunch. He would not let us eat until three P.M., claiming that was after the lunch hour. Two or three old ladies constituted the busy lunch trade.

Once in a while, I would take it upon myself to stir up the mustard cups on the tables. It was done under the close scrutiny of my father, who would always restir the cups after I finished. When a customer walked in, he would introduce me as his son and say he was training me to take over the business. I never got beyond stirring the mustard. Gulden's never called.

In my father's estimation, we were of no help at home, either. When my brother mowed the lawn, my father would mow it again. He would also wash the supper dishes, sans hot water because of the oil bill. He would walk about the house turning off lights. Even at night, I never saw him turn one on. He constantly cursed the utilities, pointing to the furnace, water faucet, telephone and lights as his arch enemies. He cursed when the phone rang, believing he was paying for incoming calls, too.

He mistrusted everyone, especially in financial transactions. "Couldn't you make it cheaper?" was his standard line on any item over a few dollars. When my mother went to a small appliance store to buy a toaster, my father cautioned her about the salesman, saying, "Watch out, he has a mustache."

When he took the family out to buy a dog, it turned into an hours-long negotiating session. The clerk placed a beagle puppy in my hands while my father bargained the price. I heard those familiar words: "Couldn't you make it cheaper?" They finally agreed, but that was not the end. With me still clutching my puppy, my father demanded that a collar be thrown into the deal. The clerk refused. My father pulled the dog from me, handed it back to the salesman with the words "Keep your stinkin' dog" and walked out the door. My tears did not reopen negotiations.

There was to be a happy ending. Driving down Jericho Turnpike, I noticed Selmer's Pet Land and I implored my father to stop. Inside we found a mixed-breed puppy, half-beagle, half everything else. The price was ten dollars. "Couldn't you make it cheaper?" my father asked. He got it for eight, collar included.

My father's frugality carried over to our summer vacations at Lake George. We stayed at a place where meals were included, and one morning my father decided he wanted extra fried eggs. The waiter told him that only one helping was allowed, so my father hid the plate and convinced the same waiter that he had not yet been served. "I'm sure I served you," the frustrated waiter said. The extra helping was brought.

One night on the vacation we went out to eat at Howard Johnson's, and my sister noticed an Elvis Presley movie was playing at a drive-in across the street. We all wanted to see the movie. So did my father, but he didn't want to pay for it. The screen was clearly visible from the restaurant's parking lot. We could see the movie, but we couldn't hear the words. "Read the lips," my father said. I called him a cheapskate and he hit me again and again. He should have read my lips after that. On another vacation we played bingo and my father kept interrupting the game and driving the number caller crazy by yelling "bingo!" every time he got one number on his playing card.

My father could turn from miser to spendthrift. He bought a Cadillac, then traded it in for a Volkswagen to save on gas. He bought a swimming pool and never went into it. He bought aluminum siding for the house, then sold the house. He sodded the front lawn, but wouldn't water it enough, so it turned brown.

When something fell into disrepair, it had to be someone's fault. When the toilet overflowed, the last one to use it was held responsible. Every stopped drain was blamed on my sister washing her hair.

My father never had a friend. He wouldn't allow himself to. He preferred enemies. We had loads of aunts and uncles but never saw them. They all carried my father's attributes. "They all thought they knew it all, and they all stunk," my mother often said. When an aunt did try to act assertive, my uncle said, "I have a mouth full of spit for you."

All of our neighbors were, in my father's estimation, no good. Good neighbor Sam he was not. To him, they either had an easier life, or had more money, or were "Jew haters." My father was not a bigot; rather, he treated everyone with contempt, not that they readily noticed it. When someone walked by the house, he would yell out, "Nice day!" and follow with some profanity under his breath.

He identified with Judaism, yet called all Jews yiddles. All non-Jews were goys. He was at best unsure about the existence of a higher authority, making him an agnostic. Mostly, he was just antagonistic.

He could deal with the neighbors better than with his family; he could turn them off by walking inside the house. But then he would have to contend with us. "I should never have had so many kids," he would say, and I, being the last one, would squirm. One child was compared to the other, all were turned against each other. The smarter brother was called Professor IQ for seeking a college education; the emotionally troubled sister was called the Nutty One; the heavier sister the Fat One and the youngest the Little One, as in too young to know anything, even into his thirties. The Little One had to help the father pack up his sister's clothes the night she was thrown out for coming home too late.

My father never played a game of catch with his sons, we never took a walk around the block, we never had our pictures taken. We rarely brought anybody to the house because my father didn't want it dirtied. When he bought a new couch, it was covered with plastic and no one was allowed to sit on it. The lampshades remained covered in plastic so they wouldn't get soiled.

I was in the next room the day of his stroke. He called to me and I rushed in to see him lying on the floor. He blamed his fall on me, for not helping him to the bathroom. The final chapter of his life had begun. He tried to adjust to life in a wheelchair, though he missed his car and the days of dealing with the car salesmen. He still dreamed of once again driving, until my mother dashed those hopes with her indelicate "What are you going to do, put a rope around your neck and pull it?"

He cracked the whip over health aides assigned for his care. They quit on the average of one a week. The minute one walked in he would order, "Quick, get the broom and sweep up." He regimented his life to the second and expected his "servants" to respond accordingly.

With my mother in failing health, both my parents were relocated to a nursing home. He called it a hotel, and he drove the staff crazy. He demanded kosher food—he had never been on such a diet before—and when he didn't like it, told the chef to "give it to Hitler." He was one of many residents in the facility, but expected to be treated as the only one. The nursing-home staff assumed his belligerence came from his illness. We knew it was just Dad being Dad. Though his body weakened, his mental faculties remained strong. His will to live lasted into his final days. The social worker hovered over his bed, telling him it was OK to let go. "No, not yet," he whispered to her.

Near the end, I made daily visits to my father. The most dominant and domineering person I will ever know was dying. Relief competed with sadness. I, who could never do anything right in his eyes, looked into his eyes. This time I wanted to be selfish, I wanted something for myself. I asked him if I had been a good son. I didn't expect an answer, but I thought I got one. He nodded his head slightly in the affirmative.

RALPH HOLCOMB

My earliest memory of my father is of him running with me across suburban lawns. I was no more than five years old then. He was happy, and happy to be with me. I felt the same. When he had the time or energy, we would play together. He often worked night shifts at the boiler plant, and so he would often be working or sleeping on afternoons and early evenings.

I soon learned that there was another darker side to him, a violent angry side that frightened me and that I think may have frightened him as well. I say this even though he was so comfortable with his child-rearing philosophy that he would jokingly say, "Hit first, ask questions later." We children even learned to laugh with him when he said it.

In my next memory I am about six years old. I was crying as I hid from my father behind the couch. My sobs gave me away. He pulled the couch away from the wall and beat me in front of the family. My mother pleaded with him (she was my defender until I could defend myself), and my older brother and sister looked shamefacedly at their shoes, quiet, knowing that if they spoke they would be next.

The next image is of my father beating me for what I believe was the last time. I was probably eight years old by then. I remember the offense: I had crossed the street without his permission. As a father myself now I can understand what probably happened. He was alone in the garage, working on one of his projects. He became too engrossed in his work, trusted my obedience too much, turned and found me gone. That is enough to send panic through any parent. That beating was significant because his blows did not hurt. I cried anyway to imitate pain and to escape him.

Shortly after this episode my mother began advising me about strategies for avoiding my father. She taught me how to bend our strict family rules without the appearance of any wrongdoing. My mother also told me about my dad. His own life was filled with fear and loss. He came from a large and poverty-stricken family. His mother died when he was just entering his teens, and his father died when he was eighteen. He entered the military before finishing high school. He had trouble expressing his love because his loved ones had been torn from him. All this I heard from my mother; my father was silent.

I never thought to ask my dad about his violence when I was young, and when I was older I refused to care anymore. I don't think my father thought of motivations anyway: hit first, ask questions later. He was guarded about his past, and the few stories he recounted seemed like they were out of an old school primer. I think he remembered his life as if it were a bad dream—the shadows passed over and he was silent again.

Another image from my middle adolescence comes to mind. I was testing out my naive liberalism by condemning Joe McCarthy, when my father began to give his own impassioned version of the communist conspiracy, ending by implicating the teachers at my school. He perceived the world as filled with danger, and people as trying to exploit him at every turn.

Some of his fears were well-founded. As I approached adolescence, my father had two heart attacks and was told to slow down or else. He had known only hard work and believed that physical exertion equaled manliness.

In my next memory, I am a lazy adolescent, twelve or thirteen. I feared and hated my father by then. Love had disappeared completely. We were in the garage, his kingdom, and I was his assistant on some job. I knew it was only a matter of time before some problem frustrated him to the point of flash anger, which would be my cue to slip back into the house to read. It was my second time out with him that day. In the morning he had been working on the car and suddenly became enraged, saying in a voice shaking with self-loathing that he couldn't see anymore, he couldn't hear anymore, he couldn't do anything. That afternoon he ordered me to do some minor chore for him. I was slow, and probably insolent in my movements (I was never insolent in words then). He blew up at me, threw his tools, and told me that I was useless for men's work and should instead learn "women's work," like doing laundry and making beds. This was strong language, even for him. I ran away to my defender, hurt and indignant. The following scene included me weeping, my father shouting, and my mother between us. There were other similar scenes, but in content they were always the same: my father shouting out his frustration at me and threatening me, my mother playing peacemaker.

I eventually learned to walk away from him, silent and filled with loathing, but at least without hiding behind my mother. Because his anger was unpredictable, I never chanced bringing friends over. We became strangers in the same house. I would sometimes bait him (as with the Joe McCarthy story) to see him break down into what I then called "temper tantrums." He lost all direct power over me by the time I turned fifteen, and I was never vulnerable with him again.

The moments of tenderness between us—and there were some—faded as any trust I had gave way to fear and then to anger. I moved away to college and then moved farther away to graduate school. We became civil to each other after a long while, silently agreeing to ignore the past. One time, when I was out for a visit, he and I were driving alone in the car. He was old by then, retired, and looking forward to some years of peace. He reached over and spontaneously grabbed my hand, saying he was sure glad to see me. I was shocked at this breach of etiquette and could only respond with mumbled platitudes. In fact I could not respond. There was nothing to bring forth. He was declaring peace, but I had left the field.

JOHN HOLVECK

I had twenty seconds or so to forgive, to ignore, or to deny absolution to this hateful man. I was not a priest, but a son; he was not a penitent, but my dad. The confessional was no cloistered corner of a church, but a Florida beach on a day of quiet winter softness.

Mom had died that February, and I came down from Pennsylvania so my father wouldn't have to spend his first widower's Easter alone. We were sitting watching the ocean when he said: "You know, I treated your mother pretty rotten."

He had, too, this vulgar, obnoxious, sometimes still abusive former alcoholic. He hadn't treated me so damn well, either. And I hated him for it.

Now he was old and sickly. I think he sensed his own mortality and wanted to come to terms with his past.

Hence, he made an admission that also implied a question. When he said, "I treated your mother pretty rotten," he was questioning whether such behavior could be forgiven. Would be forgiven by me.

He was asking if I could repeat his statement, and add on the most powerful conjunction of our moral grammar: "I was rotten, *but*. . . ." "Yes, Dad, you were rotten, but you were no worse than any other husband-father . . . but I forgive you anyway, but . . . but . . . but. . . ."

My question, then, was: Did the language my father and I spoke together, the language I learned from him, contain conjunctions or only simple sentences? I was rotten. You were rotten. Period.

From the instant he finished his admission, the meter of my conscience began running. Every second I did not answer would lead to that moment when he would conclude I did not intend to, and that would itself be an answer. If I had a different answer, it had to be given then and there.

Now he was reckless enough or desperate enough—humble enough seemed out of the question to me—to allow me to condemn him without the mercy of a qualifying "but." And to see his suffering when I did so would be a great gift.

Maybe you would have needed to see his fist knock my mother to the floor and feel the impotence of a six-year-old who had to watch it. Or to have witnessed his hurling every object in the kitchen he could get his hands on and feel an eleven-year-old's terror at the sight of it. Or to have been told that, if birth control hadn't been so much trouble, a monkey like you would never have been born.

Maybe you would have needed all of this to feel the nearly blood-lust pleasure of pronouncing the simple sentence: "Yes, Dad, you really were a bastard!" And condemn him to live out that eradicable truth for as long as he had left.

But I never said it; I chose not to deny him my personal sacrament of reconciliation. I said instead what, with my mind, with my emotions, with even my body that has its own form of truth-knowing, I believed to be a lie.

I said: "No, Dad, like all us husbands, you did good and you did bad. Don't think of yourself as rotten, Dad, just human. That's why Mom could love you, I can respect you, Our Lord will forgive you."

He kept staring out to sea, and said quietly, "Thanks." . . .

Why, then, don't I have peace? Aren't we taught that being generous and kind makes one feel good? Aren't compassion and virtue supposed to be their own reward?

So, why then did I do it? Because, on some level, I loved him and couldn't acknowledge it to myself in any other way? Or because it was the truth and, as a philosopher and teacher, who has spent life searching for and defending the little truth I could find, my reason overpowered my distorted, maybe even pathological, feelings?

Or was it like it so often is between fathers and sons? A potent and narcissistic father manipulated, even into adulthood, his son into leaving his will unchallenged and obeyed?

He willed to be forgiven; what is more, he willed to be forgiven *freely*. I forgave him. I did it freely. But did I? Or had I done what he had made me want to do, as he had since childhood, so that in the end he now has made freedom and necessity indistinguishable for me?

And is this paradox, in which we are estranged from our own freedom and which is the characteristic way of being human, the reason a fair-minded God would forgive a son's lie and a father's rottenness?

MICHAEL BLUMENTHAL

WAVING GOOD-BYE TO MY FATHER

My father, folding toward the earth again, plays
his harmonica and waves his white handkerchief
as I drive off over the hills to reclaim my life.

Each time, I am sure it's the last,
but it's been this way now for twenty-five years:
my father waving and playing "Auf Wiedersehen,"
growing thin and blue as a late-summer iris,
while I, who have the heart for love but not
the voice for it, disappear into the day, wiping
the salt from my cheeks and thinking of women.
There is no frenzy like the frenzy of his happiness,
and frenzy, I know now, is never happiness:
only the loud, belated cacophony of a lost soul
having its last dance before it sleeps forever.

The truth, which always hurts, hurts now—
I *have always wanted another father*: one
who would sit quietly beneath the moonlight,
and in the clean, quiet emanations of some
essential manhood, speak to me of what,
a kind man myself, I wanted to hear.

But this is not a poem about self-pity:

As I drive off, a deep masculine quiet rises,
of its own accord, from beneath my shoes.
I turn to watch my father's white handkerchief
flutter, like an old Hasid's prayer shawl,

among the dark clouds and the trees. I disappear
into the clean, quiet resonance of my own life.

To live, dear father, *is to forgive.*
And I forgive.

MICHEL MARRIOTT

Once, not too many years ago, I looked up from the scribble on my reporter's pad and stared into the hyperanimated face of Fidel Castro—and I saw my father. As part of a delegation of African-American journalists invited to Cuba in 1986, I counted myself lucky to be among the teeming Caribbeans crammed onto a dusty soccer field just outside a knot of empty shops, crowded flats and stands of sugarcane. Moreover, I felt a stab of surprise that I had somehow stepped, flesh and blood, into my father's dream.

Long disenchanted with what he called the "trick bag" of the United States, my father reveled in the sheer bravado of the Cuban revolution, its elevation of the Brown and Black to real power. He often talked, half jokingly, of course, of retiring someday to that island republic and having Uncle Sam send his Social Security checks to Havana.

In recognition of the special significance my journey might hold for him, I presented Dad with a gift on my return. To my disappointment, however, he barely accepted the carefully framed photograph I had taken of Castro and inscribed with words of tribute to my father's courage as a freethinker.

Why is it so difficult for us? I asked myself some weeks later when I discovered the picture pitched against a mound of disarray on my father's desk. After so many years of being buffeted by swirling currents of father-son tensions, intermittent hostilities and redeeming love, *why*, I mused, *does it remain so hard for us—two Black men—to, well, just get along?* There had been times when we had hurled hurtful words at each other like poison-tipped spears. We had even, in dizzying and terrifying fits of machismo, both reached for guns, prepared to shoot each other if need be.

Why wasn't it like television, where dads wore suits and ties to the dinner table and were ever ready to lend an ear or dispense fatherly advice with a knowing grin? Where was Fred MacMurray in blackface?

The truth is that for millions of Black men, our relationships with our fathers represent lifetimes of unfinished business. Much too often our most obvious models—from whom we begin to fashion our distinctive sense of a masculine identity—are marginal to our lives because of our fathers' physical or emotional absence from home. . . .

For example, my father would bristle with indignation whenever he discovered my brother and me, as young boys, watching Saturday-morning cartoons. "You don't have time for that bullshit," he'd say in a tone so sharp our child-joy would expire on the spot. "The white man wants you to look at Bugs Bunny while he's figuring out better ways to beat you. You better learn some math, read a book."

There'd be no hugs given or "good mornings" spoken. There was always so much harshness, a sternness very much like that I saw years later captured in Troy Maxson's rage and reason in August Wilson's play *Fences*. When Troy's teenage son, Cory, asks him why he doesn't like him, Troy responds with fury: "I done give you everything I had to give you. I gave you your life! Me and your mama worked that out between us. And liking your black ass wasn't part of the bargain. Don't you try and go through life worrying about if somebody like you or not. You best be making sure they doing right by you." Similarly, growing up with my father, at the time a factory worker at a synthetic-rubber manufacturing plant in Louisville, Kentucky, was like growing up in boot camp, training for the inevitable clashes with white racism and domination that waited just outside the nest of our segregated neighborhood.

Yet I identified with my father. I marveled at his strength—not merely muscular, since he was never a particularly large man. I was in awe of his accordionlike ability to expand on demand, to pump up his nerve and face down anyone who threatened him or his wife or three boys, whether a landlord, a police officer or a teacher who shirked responsibility. In that way, among many, I wanted to be like him: smart, tough, the relentless warrior. . . .

I love my father. Some of that love stems from my culture's obligation to honor him because he is my father. Yet another, much larger, part of that love flows from my understanding of him, my empathy with his life and wounds as a proud Black man dangling from a leafless tree of opportunities denied. At sixty-three, my father is a man of enormous talents and, in his own estimation, of humble accomplishments. Many demons still stir in his soul.

For the past ten years we have moved, gently, to resolve our conflicts, to settle into roles reassigned to us by time and growth. In the last few years he has let me hug him when I see him now, which is all too infrequently. I, on the other hand, have reined in my juvenile urges to compete with him, to prove in battles of wit and wile that I am as much a man as he is.

For the last three years I've pulled out the same card of bright colors and upbeat prose I bought for Father's Day. But each year something prevents me from sending it. Procrastination abounds, moving me to return the card to my top drawer, more determined to actually send it to him the next year. Yet, as I wrote this article in the late summer, a process that forced me to refocus my feelings about Pop, I got out the card, signed it "I love you" and sent it homeward. I hope its arrival, though odd, will signal to him anew my homage to our connections, both involuntary and voluntary, both of the blood and of the heart.

I want my father to know that with each morning look into the bathroom mirror, I see a little more of his face peering through mine. Life's journey is circular, it appears. The years don't carry us away from our fathers—they return us to them.

5

Reunion

LEE THOMAS / LAWRENCE WRIGHT
DEAN PITCHFORD / BILL MOYERS
PAT JORDAN / RONALD FORSYTHE
JIM GALLAGHER / FREDERICK MANNING
JOHN ED BRADLEY / GEORGE EYRE MASTERS

LEE THOMAS

It wasn't until I talked with my father as an adult that I truly got to know him. As a child I had many questions about why he said the things and did the things he did. I'd be so angry at him that all I could think of was which way he should die.

My father was solidly built and quick, like a defensive linebacker. His thick hands felt like vise grips, and people often remarked on their strength. His olive-green eyes were bright against his reddish-brown skin. When he looked at you, his piercing eyes locked on to yours like radar on a homing beacon, and he didn't blink.

My father was a dictator in his house, and his word was law. "Don't do as I do, do as I say," he would often remark. If you disobeyed, punishment was swift and sometimes harsh. Some of the beatings I got would be considered child abuse by today's standards.

He beat me once on a snowy Christmas Day when I was about twelve. My younger brother and I were playing a new game I had gotten, and when I caught him cheating, I scolded him. He got mad, so we started yelling at each other. Dad's solution to that was to whip both of us, because arguing wasn't permitted in *his* house. Later he offered me money to buy myself something. It was his way of apologizing. But to have heard him say "I'm sorry" or to have him give me a hug would have been worth more than anything else. "It is difficult for your daddy to apologize," my mother told me. She didn't say why, but I guessed it was for the same reason he didn't hug her.

Living at home was hard sometimes. My father did exactly what he wanted, at everyone else's expense. When I or anyone else was watching television, he would turn the channel if a program was on that he wanted to see. Especially football. If more than one game was on, he'd monopolize both our televisions.

Often when I asked permission to do something, he'd say no and offer no explanations. Fortunately, my mother was there to comfort me. She advised me to study him and learn to understand his moods in order to get what I wanted. I didn't realize it then, but that's what she had done.

But even after I understood how to maneuver around his difficult ways, I still wondered what made him that way: Why was he so domineering and self-centered? Why couldn't he be more kind, more considerate of the feelings of others, more lovable? I knew he had it in him because it would sometimes slip out: He would unexpectedly show up with flowers for my mother or take the family to a movie.

The answer to some of my questions came much later, when he had aged and mellowed, and I was an adult, single and independent. We were having light conversation alone at the kitchen table. My father mentioned some past incident involving me and the family that he fondly recalled. That's when the tears started to fill my eyes. I tried my best to hold them back, but the more I tried, the more they came. I didn't share his happy view of the past. Years of pent-up feelings and memories gushed forth, pouring from my eyes. No dam in the world could hold them back and I knew it was time, time to talk about the past. No more holding it in. I loved my father and I was going to let him know how I had felt all these years.

I told him everything that had bothered me about him from my childhood on. He was surprised that I remembered so much. He listened patiently as I poured out my feelings. This was a milestone because he hadn't listened much when I was younger. After I was done he spoke.

He told me about his childhood and how tough it had been growing up poor in rural southern New Jersey. He was raised by his mother, a strong, domineering woman, and his stepfather. His natural father, who had only a third-grade education, abandoned the family when my father was very young. It was very important to my father that he be a good provider, unlike his own dad.

After his description of life when he was growing up, I understood him better. At the time there were definite ideas about how men and women should be. Men worked, women took care of the home. Real men didn't cry or have any outward display of emotion.

During our talk we reached a level of intimacy and communication that had never existed between us before. While I didn't agree with his reasoning on some matters, at least I knew why he felt the way he did. This made a big difference.

I've forgiven my dad for things he did in the past. Forgiveness is a powerful thing. It paves the way for relationships to grow. As a result, my dad and I are closer now than ever. We've even started hugging each other, and each time it gets easier for him to do.

I finally have the kind of relationship with him that I've always wanted. He's not just my father anymore. He's my friend.

LAWRENCE WRIGHT

When my son, Gordon, was three, he saw his first gorilla. The gorilla cast him an indifferent look and went back to watching "General Hospital" on the color TV just outside his cage. I was holding Gordon, and when we got outside, he wanted to walk alone.

That night Gordon had a nightmare. "Big monkey in the sky!" he kept screaming as my wife tried to calm him. "Bang on my head with a hammer!"

He was, I realized, dreaming about me. All week I had been doing carpentry work in the basement underneath Gordon's room. When I was a boy, my own father and I spent many hours in another basement refinishing furniture, and it gave me a lifelong taste for woodworking. Those were the hours when I felt closest to my father, when I had him all to myself. It was an experience I was eager to pass along to my son. But he was afraid of power tools. Loud noises frightened him. In his room, safely away from the violence of my basement construction, he still complained about my hammering. I could see myself as he had imagined me in his dream: a menacing ape with a hammer in his hand, a creature of fear and punishment, a simian Jehovah. I knew then that Gordon would love me with the same fear and intensity with which I loved my father, for a boy's father is, after all, his first competitor and his eternal enemy.

I remember vividly my father's gait. He took giant strides, and I had to run to stay in step. He was big; his voice was deep. I admired the way he sang in church. In the shower he would sing "Marie, the dawn is breaking" without knowing all the words and "K-K-K-Katie . . . I'll be waiting at the k-k-k-kitchen door" and all the wonderful songs of the big band, wartime era. He gave me "whisker kisses" when he needed a shave. He punished me when I misbehaved. He was strict, sometimes harsh, usually merciful, always fair. I think it was his fairness that I feared most.

He was an infantry officer in World War II and came home eager to have children. I arrived in the first wave of the baby boom; two sisters quickly followed. I have often wondered why the urge to procreate, which was so pronounced in his generation, should be so stunted in my own. Perhaps it has something to do with the wars each generation has had to fight. All wars are horrible, but men who fight in a just cause become heroes. He was such a hero. I would never be.

We spent much of my childhood and all of my adolescence in a prolonged and canny combat—for that's how it is with fathers and sons; they are bound to grapple with each other, to test their wills, to compete. Boys naturally fear their fathers and envy them. The father sets limits; the son rebels. The father is stronger, but time and nature favor the son.

History—especially American history—is a long story of sons' overturning their progenitors. The battle of the generations began in our country with the American Revolution against "Papa" George III and continued in my generation with the reaction against Vietnam. By then my father and I were bloody veterans of my rebellion. We would stand in the living room blazing away at each other like the *Monitor* and the *Merrimack*, giving no quarter, asking none, both of us furious, inflexible, verbally skilled, and ruthless.

But neither of us was prepared for the savagery of the war at home—certainly the most divisive episode in the long saga of American families. One could feel the generations peeling apart. However angry my father and I might have been in the past, we were now irreconcilable. It was a subject we knew to avoid, and yet neither of us could leave it alone. All family gatherings deteriorated into the same grinding argument: duty versus conscience. Our ethics made us savage. On the day I graduated from college— the day I became eligible for the draft—we had a showdown in the hotel parking lot. It was a fight we had been expecting for quite a long time, and no weapon would fail to be used. What I remember most about the encounter is the cruel pleasure we took in this final bloodletting, as Mother wailed helplessly for us to stop, to leave some love in the family. But of course we couldn't stop; we had been building toward it since the moment of my conception. There was an Old Testament glory in our willingness to play out the tragedy of fathers and sons to its bitter conclusion. I left the U.S. soon after that, as a conscientious objector. By then my country and my father were one and the same to me.

It is one of the surprises of life that a son turns out to love his father after all. Two years abroad took the heat out of our relationship. I was married and on my own, but the preoccupations of my life gradually took on a familiar character—they were my father's hobbies and enthusiasms, his traits, his failings, rubbed into my grain like an oil stain on one of the cabinets we refinished in my youth, rubbed in, moreover, with real force, with elbow grease, so that the stain would sink deeply into my pores and my life would always be colored by his influence.

When Gordon was born, my father and I were reconciled, in a cautious fashion. There is a time when all fathers must surrender, a time when their sons no longer think of them and the battle becomes moot. As for the sons, they grow up and get their own punishment.

Would I ever be as good a father to Gordon as my father was to me? It was not a question I would have thought to ask myself some years earlier, although there was a time in my life (I now remembered) when I believed I had the very best father in the world—the strongest, the bravest, the fairest. The fear I had upon becoming a father myself was that a man could be all those things to his son and still be his enemy. But isn't that a father's highest, noblest duty to his son? To be his son's friendly foe? To create the man who will better him? To teach him and prod him and discipline him? To challenge him and make him work beyond himself? To beat him sometimes at his favorite games so that he can feel the bite of competition? To make him stand up for what he believes in—even when, one day, what his son believes in may break his heart? And finally, finally, to show him how to lose, as all fathers must lose if they are successful, for what man wishes for a son who is not his superior?

Just after Gordon was born, I stood looking at him through the glass of the hospital nursery. He was red-faced and bawling. At nearly ten pounds and 22½ inches long, he was the biggest baby born all week (he would certainly be bigger than me). We would play catch together. We would fish. I would take him camping. We would build things together in the basement. I would give him the love and attention my father gave me, and no doubt he would give me in turn what I gave my father.

At that moment I noticed my father's reflection in the glass. He had come up behind me and was standing there watching his son. Almost immediately I began boasting—the proud father myself now—about Gordon's size, his obvious good looks, his brilliant future. My father smiled. He recalled that his own son had been a big baby.

Not as big as my baby.

I said it aloud, a thought I let slip before I had fully handled its absurdity. I was still competing, still comparing my accomplishments with my father's, and I had thoroughly bested him this time. My baby is bigger than your baby, but your baby was . . . me.

And we laughed together, two wise old fathers in the presence of life's new rebel.

DEAN PITCHFORD

In all the time I was growing up, I never heard my father speak about what it was like to have been at Pearl Harbor on December 7, 1941. He showed us photographs instead. He had grown up in the Hawaiian Islands, traveled to New York City to study photography with Margaret Bourke-White, then returned to Hawaii as a Navy photographer. When the bombs fell, he witnessed the whole thing through a viewfinder, becoming one of the few to capture the onslaught on film.

My earliest memories of my father always include his cameras—and the unwieldy assortment of lenses and flash units, cables and flare guards that went along with them back then. He maintained scrapbooks on me and my two brothers, filled, it seemed to me, with moments that most children would rather forget. My every move, every discovery, seemed to get taken from me and engraved in silver nitrate: my first bottle, my first pancake, my first day of school, my first holy communion. No important moment escaped his camera. Sometimes he would run out into the yard as we played ball and order us to turn this way or that. "O.K., that was good. Just one more." "Aw, Daddy, that was *already* 'just one more!' " "I know, I know. But give me just one more."

We always obliged.

My father had a darkroom at the factory where he worked as an industrial photographer, but he built one into our house as well. After dinner, he would disappear for hours into that air-conditioned amber-lighted box. At bedtime, after we had said our prayers with my mother, we three boys would line up, knock on the door and wait for him to unlatch it. Covered with an apron, his hands in wet rubber gloves, he would present his cold cheek for us to kiss goodnight.

Early every November, the family would assemble for our annual greeting card. For an entire afternoon, we would fidget and whine as Dad set the camera on a tripod, focused endlessly, triggered the timer, then ran back to join us in familial merriment just before the flash detonated. As we all blinked away the purple-green spot of flash, he would race back to reset the timer. Over and over and over. My mother used those moments to swipe at our brilliantined hair with a brush she would tuck out of sight between shots. I would ask why we couldn't send store-bought cards, like everybody else.

In the photo that was finally picked, we always looked like the ideal family, a perfect pose.

The day after I graduated from eighth grade, my father left home and my family stopped taking pictures. My mother bought an Instamatic, which she occasionally remembered to pull out before someone blew out the candles on a birthday cake; but the film would remain in the camera, undeveloped.

For almost seventeen years, communication between me and my father was limited to birthday cards and Christmas cards—store-bought, with his name stamped in gold, never signed. He never had been one for words; and, as the years slipped away, I figured he had less and less to say anyway.

Several years ago, I visited my mother at home in Hawaii. In flipping through my old scrapbook, I found a photo taken one Thanksgiving. The family is gathered around the dining table, and, in the center of the snapshot, my father's chair sits empty; he, of course, was taking the picture. That empty chair haunted me. In examining all the prints carefully, I found that my father hardly appears in a single picture; and yet I realize his presence in every one of them. I could sense him. He's the one we were all smiling for.

Then, continuing through the scrapbook, I found empty black pages where my adolescence was supposed to have been chronicled. I wondered, if he had been present, what images my father would have captured on film. The photo opportunities had passed. For lack of evidence, I felt almost as if the years had never been lived. Suddenly, I missed those pictures, I missed my father's peculiar way of snatching moments and preserving emotions. I missed the silent give-and-take that each picture implied. I missed him.

I sat down and wrote him a very long letter, detailing seventeen years of my life. Six weeks passed. He wrote back —a cautious note accompanied by snapshots of his retirement party, of his new life in the mountains of California, of the darkroom he had built into his two-bedroom trailer home. I responded with newsy accounts of my career. He replied with more photos.

Gradually, he began supplementing his pictures with written accounts of his activities. His letters told of a dusty bus trip across Baja California, a cruise to Venezuela, castles in Spain.

He developed cataracts, and, while he waited for the operation to remove them, he began to telephone. Those conversations led comfortably to the first of his many visits.

My father still arrives with cases of cameras, tripods, filters, lenses, batteries and film. He photographs my house and the street and the trees and the sun rising and setting, from my rooms. His photos show me my world in a different light. But when he urges me to sit and smile for him, I generally decline. I no longer want him looking at me with his photographer's eye, taking without giving back.

Instead, I get him to sit for me . . . and to tell me about things that we never even broached when I was growing up. Because there is no camera in front of his face, I can see his eyes. He squints into the past and tries to envision the scenes anew.

In carefully measured phrases, he talks about adventures I had not dreamed were within his experience: of being a cabin boy at sixteen aboard a sailing ship that carried lumber from Washington state to Hawaii in the late 1920s; of witnessing a fight between an Indian Sikh and a Chinese peasant in Shanghai in 1934 that ended with the Indian's drawing his sword and beheading his adversary; of watching the bombs fall on Pearl Harbor. I sit and listen in awe to his meticulous re-creations of these dramas. In the pictures that he describes to me, my father is always there, sharp and in focus. After so many years of standing out of frame and capturing other people's stories on glossy stock, he is no longer just the camera. He is, at last, the subject— revealing himself to me, providing the most indelible images of him I will ever have.

BILL MOYERS

When I was born in 1934 my father was making two dollars a day working on the construction of a new highway from the Texas border to Oklahoma City. We were living in the southeastern corner of Oklahoma in an area known as "Little Dixie" because so many people had come there from Arkansas, Texas, Louisiana, Mississippi and Alabama.

I have not spent any time in Oklahoma for years, although my childhood impressions were sharply etched in my mind and I have always felt that men like my father, coming to maturity in the '20s and laid low by the '30s, were a special lot; they were born before Oklahoma was admitted to the Union and the state took shape around their labors and losses. They had no option but to cope, and their experiences fueled a whole generation's determination not to repeat them. . . .

I went back last week and the memories were still there. My father, who is seventy now, came up on the bus from Texas and we drove from Oklahoma City down through familiar parts of the state. . . .

A late afternoon sun the size of a prospector's imagination was hanging in the sky as we drove out to their old farm. We turned off on a levee along the Washita River that Uncle Harry had built with a team of mules; in those days he and my father and men like them qualified to vote in local elections by helping to build country roads—two days of work to qualify if they brought a mule, five if not. "There was a time during the Depression when the only meat we had to eat was jackrabbits we caught in the fields," my father said. "And sometimes," Uncle Harry added, "we'd run alongside 'em to feel their ribs to see if they were fat enough t'cook." . . .

My father's parents married in Tahlequah, in what was then Indian Territory, and moved south of the Red River into Texas, to farm the waxy black land. Grandfather died of pneumonia in 1916 and two years later the family returned to Oklahoma with a new stepfather. They owned four mules and two wagons, a buckboard buggy, two milk cows, two calves, a pig and some chickens. The January weather was cold and wet and it took them two days to travel thirty miles. After they had ferried the Red River near Frogville the two young mules got stuck in the muddy bottom land, became excited and scared trying to get out, and turned the wagon over into the muck. My father, who was then twelve, and his brother Harry tried to recover some of grandmother's canned fruits but they failed.

They settled in Choctaw County, not far from where the "Trail of Tears" had ended years earlier for the Chickasaw, Choctaw, Cherokee, Seminole and Creek Indians who had been forcibly removed by the U.S. Government from their old lands in the Deep South. Sadness and hardship were the lot of most people, red men and white, who tried to impose their hope on the realities of nature in this part of the country, and the incident on the Red River was only a harbinger of difficult times to come. Men swore and watched helplessly as it rained when they didn't want it and didn't when they desperately needed it. Their wives cooked on wood stoves and washed clothes in black pots and buried children who couldn't survive the diphtheria and malaria and bore more who did; twin daughters born to my mother both died, one of whom might have been saved had there been a doctor or medicine nearby. When flu and pneumonia struck, people wrapped asafetida gum in a cloth around the necks of their ailing kin and waited, often in vain.

In the winter they shook with the cold and in the summer they sweltered. My father and his brother used to scoop fifteen tons of cottonseed a day from a wagon onto a conveyor belt, in 110 degrees, for fifty cents a ton each. That was a temporary job when the gins were running and the rest of the time they tried to farm, always on another man's land—fourteen hours a day behind a team of mules. My father wanted to stay with farming but he had to give up shortly before I was born. He had expected to get half a bale of cotton to the acre on thirty-five acres, but it rained all of July and half of August and the boll weevils came like an Old Testament plague and it was over; he went to work on the highway. Eventually he got a job driving a truck for a creamery—fifteen dollars and expenses for a six-day week —and we moved to Texas. One by one his own brothers —except for Uncle Harry—left the land, migrating to California and into the pages of a Steinbeck novel.

In recapturing the past last week, we were not trying to do so in some idealized way, to make things what they never were, nor to escape; a seventy-year-old man who has buried four of his five children doesn't extol the good old days, and I still have places to be. We were looking, instead, for landmarks to share again after years of separate journey, and in ordinary places, while there was still time, we found them.

PAT JORDAN

My mother and father had been with us for only two days when I had my first argument with Dad. We had been arguing constantly, it seemed, for more than forty years. That's why I had invited them, in their late seventies, to come down from Connecticut to stay with me and my wife in our new home in Florida for a few days in winter. To make my peace, finally, with the old man.

After the argument, I called my brother back in Connecticut. "Jeez," I said, "the old man's still a pain in the ass."

"Why can't you get along with him?" my brother said. He is thirteen years older than me.

"I'm trying! I'm trying! But he drives me nuts!"

"Forget it already. Listen, why don't you take the old man out. Just you and him. Go shoot some pool. You know how you used to love to shoot pool with him."

"All right."

I took Dad out to a bar-pool-hall out on Dixie Highway, near the body shops and the auto parts stores. A red-neck sort of place just over the railroad tracks. I parked in a gravel lot between a pickup truck that looked like it had been repainted with a brush and an orange Chevelle Super Sport with racing slicks and rusted mag wheels. I heard country music through the open door. It was dark inside. It smelled of urine and baby powder and stale beer. I went over to the barmaid, who was talking to a fat, bearded guy with a clip of keys hanging from the belt loop of his oil-stained jeans. She seemed deliberately not to notice me and Dad. I waited at the bar. Dad stood by the door, a small, tentative old man fingering his hat in his hands. Finally, the barmaid came over to me. I asked for a rack of balls.

She gestured with her head toward Dad. "For you and pops, huh?" She had teased black hair like straw.

"Yeah," I said with a smile. "The old man shoots a pretty mean stick."

"I'll bet, honey." She handed me the balls. "Take your pick." She gestured toward the six deserted Brunswick tables.

My father and I went over to one of the tables and turned on the conical light above it. Dad ran the flat of his hand over the green felt. He shook his head. We got pool cues from racks along the walls. Dad laid his cue stick flat on the table and rolled it over the felt. It wobbled. He got another. That one wobbled, too. He got another and another until finally he got one that didn't wobble. I racked the balls.

"A game of straight, Dad?" I said. He nodded. I played a safety. The cue ball stopped at one end of the table and only one ball broke free from the rack at the other end. I'd left him a long, straight-in shot. It was a tough shot, but it could be made. Dad went over to the barmaid and said something. She reached under the bar and handed him a container of Johnson's baby powder. He sprinkled it on his hands and returned to the table. He examined the balls quickly, bent low over the cue ball and sighted his shot.

He had short, fat fingers. Not a pool shooter's hands. My mother called them "sausage fingers." Like she threw in the spaghetti sauce, she said. I watched Dad grip the stick. He still had that firm lefthander's bridge, though, even at seventy-six, and that smooth stroke that I always tried to copy but never could. Dad shot and missed. The cue ball broke into the rack and scattered the balls. I had a dozen easy shots to choose from. I remembered what Dad had told me once. "The eyes go before the stroke," he had said. That was almost twenty years ago. I was a pretty fair shooter then. I used to play every day after class at a pool hall in town, near the college I attended. I always won a few dollars from the other students. But I could never beat Dad. We would play for hours. I would get sweaty and hot-tempered as I watched him, cool-eyed, with that maddeningly methodical stroke, pocket ball after ball without missing. The other students stood around and watched my father shoot. I was both proud of Dad's talent and furious that I could not beat him. More than anything then, I wanted to beat him in pool. Not to embarrass him but to show him how good I was, at his game. . . .

After only a few racks it became obvious that Dad's eyes were gone. I had built up a big lead, playing hard and ruthless. The way Dad had played me when I was in college. He never let up on me. Never gave me a break the way some fathers do. I wouldn't have had it any other way. The thought of him deliberately missing a shot so that I could win would have made me sick. It was a good lesson. But it never really took. I could play hard and ruthless only for a while. It was an act, really, that I could never sustain. I didn't feel it. The hardness. I was not single-minded about my purpose, any purpose, no matter what.

I stepped back from the pool table and blinked. I shook my head to clear it. I was ahead by more than twenty balls. Dad was standing there, leaning on his stick, an old man with a gray fringe of hair at his temples, waiting for me to shoot. I leaned over the table, took an almost impossible shot, and missed. The balls scattered over the green felt.

"What the hell's a' matter with you?" he said. "You know better than that." I shrugged, shook my head as if disgusted with myself. Dad leaned over the table and ran out the rack. I racked the balls again. "That's what happens when you get careless," he said.

When Dad finally missed again I missed my next shot by hitting the object ball just hard enough to make it pop out of the pocket after it had dropped in. "You've got a touch like a blacksmith," Dad said.

I lost the game to my father by three balls. I threw my arm over the old man's shoulders and said, "Dad, you're still the best."

"You shoulda beat me," he said. "You got careless." He looked up at me and shook his head as if truly sad. "As usual."

I returned the balls to the barmaid and paid the bill. She smiled at me. "The old man took you to the cleaners, huh?" she said.

I looked around for Dad. He was over by the door, out of earshot. "I let him win," I said.

"Sure you did. Sure you did."

I smiled.

That night my parents and my wife and I ate dinner on the deck outside our apartment, which overlooks the Intra-coastal Waterway. It was a warm, soft Florida night in February. My wife had lighted candles enclosed in glass. The sky was the color of purple plums, dotted here and there with white stars. A breeze blew up from the ocean. Boats rocked in the water. I raised a glass of red wine and said, "A toast! To Mom and Dad!" Their faces were illuminated by the flickering lights of the candles. We all clicked our glasses over the table heaped with food. Me. My wife. My mother. My father.

"Who won, son?" my mother said. I looked at her as we all began to eat. "In pool," she added. "Did you beat Dad?"

I smiled. "Are you kidding, Ma? You know I can't beat the old man."

Dad stopped eating. "He got careless, Florence," he said. "He had me beat and then he began taking these crazy shots."

"Oh," she said. "You mean, Patty let you win." My father looked at her and then he looked at me.

"You sonuvabitch!" he said to me. "You *did* let me win."

"Come on, Dad. I've been trying to beat you for years. You think I finally get you on the ropes and I'm gonna go in the tank?" I shook my head.

"You sonuvabitch!" My father nodded his head, a series of little nods, and then he smiled at me for the first time since he'd arrived in Florida.

RONALD FORSYTHE

The projector couldn't be lying: There, moving in 8mm, was my twenty-nine-year-old father, pushing me along the sidewalk in some kind of kiddie stroller, a look of parental concern—and pride—on his face. Was this the childhood monster I remembered?

Nonagenarian Great-Uncle Harry had recently sent me the film, a tiny composite one-reeler he had done of me from age one on, whenever I'd visited the aunts, uncles, and grandparents (Dad's mom and dad) in hilly southeastern Ohio.

And there was Dad, again, lifting a wriggling me toward the camera lens—and grinning! Was this the angry ogre, the ghoulish nightmare figure who made me gay? The man who turned upon, then finally away from, me?

But, hold on, I told myself. I *did* recall, I *had* known a harsh, bitter-tongued, grim-faced father, too. A man whom Uncle Harry had not captured, or had not wanted to. The film showed me only a young, caring father I thought had never existed.

Immediately, I wondered: What made him change, made him become the childhood horror (and later the stranger) I'd known? I recalled his dour disapproval of anything "feminine" I did, his flare-ups of temper—and how soon all this had begun. How very soon. . . .

Every relationship is a two-way proposition. Even one between parent and child—in which the former is, granted, generally light-years ahead of the latter in wisdom. But, I ask myself, can the child, despite his disadvantage, determine the way in which the relationship will develop?

In none of my very early life—three, four, five, and six years of age—was I ever able to let myself be at ease with my father. But, though he was no beau idéal of a dad—and frequent ugly confrontations with Mama struck my too-ready ears, revealed his too-volatile temper—he made real forays to reach an evasive me. The film and other photographs I've kept document some of his attempts. And I remember, now. But soon would come the quarrels and disagreements, his frustration when I didn't meet his image of what a son should be, the accusations that Mama was making me a sissy, the uncontrollable fury, and finally the neglect. We would become strangers who lived together.

I believe we had been strangers from a very early time on, however. I feel certain today that even in the first, formative, walking-and-talking years, when Dad *was trying,* I was pulling away. Maybe by an absolute excess of tenderness on his part I would have grown close to him and more closely like him. Had he even luckily been capable of such an approach, I nevertheless believe that I already had something subtly different going for me, something by now at work in me, that would forever prevent an identification with him and would chart Dad's ugly course *re* me. This budding differentness could not allow me to fully relate to him. It made me fearful and shy of him, made me deny him.

He must have sensed, as well as seen, that denial; that, even when I'd gone along with him to the Saturday-afternoon ballgame, I was not really in the ballpark. Any sensitive father must surely at last comprehend that he is not truly trusted, or admired—or wanted. This comprehension, this startling discovery, must confuse at first. Then hurt. Terribly.

On my sixth Christmas, the undersized football that Dad ("Daddy," then) had given me lay unkicked, untossed, in a corner of the wrappings-strewn living room. On my seventh, the toy tank sat neglected under the decorated fir tree. Then, finally, on my eighth, the sled had been welcome (it held no purely boy connotations for me?), though Dad would have preferred to see me ride it belly-bumper instead of seated upright—more safely, *I* thought.

Still, things didn't seem quite right to him. One summer, he came out with it point-blank: "Why don't you play with boys, or at least boys your own age? Billy is too young for you." I had invited Betty and Lois and Billy-from-down-the-street into the backyard to use the sliding-board and swings. "They'll start calling you 'sissy,' at school next fall," Dad warned, and was right. Could I answer him that I did not like the boys he meant, had discovered that they did not like me, and that the rough games they played seemed inane compared to the Nancy Drew and Hardy Boys mysteries I had begun to read, the long hikes I took down to the creek with little Billy and my dog Butch, the vegetables I'd planted in the Victory Garden or the phlox and nicotianas I'd seeded along the back fence, my shopping expeditions with another pal, Aunt Nell, the Ravel and Debussy recordings Billy's mother played for me?

He made one last-ditch attempt, when I was nine or ten. He took me and Billy down to the school softball diamond, found some other small boys there whom we knew, and pitched for us. We did this several times, and softball *was* fun, especially the running, for my legs were long and limber. But though I grew to like him more, I did not grow more like him. Especially when he wanted me to listen with him to the droning summer-afternoon baseball games on our radio set. Or when some of his men-friends joined us on the diamond, or nasty-mouthed older boys horned in, and made it a grim "professional" contest rather than simple play. It was then that I left them and went home.

He was soon to grow surly with me. The war was on, and he worked a grueling night shift at Curtiss-Wright, just outside Columbus, where we lived; an alcoholism, acquired in Depression days, increased at what he thought was my mother's unfaithfulness; Dad's mother, never a real friend to Mama (who had taken her son away to the Big City), may have prodded—or at least had not discouraged—those suspicions.

But Mama herself thoughtlessly fanned the flames: She worked, evenings, at her father's bar/restaurant, two blocks away from our house, and had a variety of men- as well as women-friends there. Furthermore, by this moonlighting she saw more of her father than she did of her husband. Mama adored her jovial, popular dad—much more than she did her quiet, old-fashioned mother. My own dad, I began to notice, was becoming increasingly jealous; his face told me. Worse, why and when I ever began to call Mama's affectionate father "Daddy Jess," rather than "Grandad" or "Grandaddy," I'll never know. It must have shamed and hurt Dad to think that I needed another. In addition, Dad had some deep-seated dislike of Mama's mother; I believe he thought she disapproved of his drinking and would have preferred that my mother divorce him—but his suspicions were, I'm thoroughly convinced, wrong. Oh, we were one big happy family! What's more, to add insult to injury, the bar/restaurant was doing a land-office business in those hectic war years and made my father, as well as his small-town parents, seem poor by comparison with their affluent big-city in-laws.

Meanwhile, I alienated Dad further by becoming Mama's almost-constant companion.

Mama—and my unalloyed happiness with her—deserve some description. A mere five-foot-one, she drove the family Nash like a racing champ, could park it on a dime, and thumbed her nose at any impatient male who wanted to honk her through a yellowing traffic light. How many nights we jumped into the car to drive across town to see Barbara Stanwyck or Ida Lupino or Ann Sheridan—away from Dad, who disliked movies—just she and I on an adventure of our own, her plumpish, skilled hands on the wheel, the scent of her cologne and feel of her jersey dress comforting to me, like the dark and bouncy front seat with its warm-lighted dash and Harry James's horn wailing out of the car radio, as we 35-mile-an-hour'ed it (she chafing at the wartime limit) to a parking spot around the corner from the flashing marquee, bought two tickets and the inevitable bags of popcorn, and plunged into adjoining seats just in time to hear the MGM lion growl for the first feature!

Mama's estrangement from Dad was paralleling my own estrangement from him. One night, she and I had returned from the movies and I'd gone to bed. Hearing her sudden scream, I scrambled up again and ran downstairs to the kitchen. My father sat astride her on the floor, slapping and punching her face. A chair was overturned, a cup lay broken on the linoleum. "Daddy, stop!" I pleaded. "Stop, oh *stop!* Don't hurt Mama! *Don't!*" He stared at me, silent, a defeated competitor for her affections, then rose and staggered, half-drunk, into the dining room.

For months afterward, speech was impossible between us and our eyes seldom met. I might have forgiven him had he sought me out and have always wondered whether he might have done so with a heterosexual son or with a daughter; but he had a different type of son—one who would not, could not, emulate him, and one whose psychic makeup created a broader gap from him than generation. Well, it was up to him to make the step toward reconciliation, I told myself. Or toward, at least, that armed truce that was our ordinary. I say "I might have forgiven him . . ." because, although I had begun to fear him, I wanted very much for him to love me and wanted to be unafraid to love him—without duplicating him. To love him *as me.* But he must certainly have believed that I had by now chosen sides, had disavowed him. From this time on, there would be little contact and virtually no real communication. Even before Mama died.

It was the following year, and it was as abrupt as it was unexpected. She made a quick call to Dad, at work, in the wee hours; was rushed to the hospital in agony, her painkillers ("Painkillers?" we all asked incredulously) having run out that evening; and what she'd avoided telling anybody, perhaps even herself, came to light. An operation . . . a few days in the hospital, with cancer . . . then peritonitis . . . then the end. My pal, my mother, was gone.

When her parents moved in with Dad and me to keep house for us, I quite literally thanked God. I could never have envisioned living alone with my father because, besides being strangers, I blamed him for my mother's death; he had been, I was so childishly certain, the true reason.

So my Life with Father luckily ended before it began. And, next—wonder of wonders!—a year later, with Dad's sullen consent, my mother's parents took this twelve-year-old away, in their retirement to Florida, to grow up in their care. Neither Dad nor I wept at our separation. Or so I believed.

Down south, even though I immediately earned the monicker "Dam' Yankee," I soon learned to you-all it with the best of the species Florida Cracker. I was soon gaining confidence in myself as a hardworking student and as a church and school vocalist to compensate for the lack of sports interest and achievement that disappointed Daddy Jess, who, however, quickly came to understand—or at least accept and respect—his oddish grandson. My confidence, and new happiness, also erased some of the fear I had kept of my father. To wit: Once, Dad mailed me a ten-dollar check, along with a note hinting that if my grand-father was niggardly (which D.J. wasn't), *he* was not. I sent the check back, instructing Dad to watch his language when speaking about my generous grandparents. Whatever I was, so unlike most of the boys I knew—and I knew nothing about either homosexuality *or* sexuality at this point—I was beginning to like what I was, and would soon offer no apologies to my father, or anybody, about myself.

In the years that followed, there were duty visits to Dad when we three returned north to Ohio each summer. Icy contacts. I was determined to remain independent and aloof; my father was curious about his changing son but undemonstrative, only irascible at any touch of gentleness he saw or heard in me. For I was now my grandmother's boy, he saw, as I had once been my mama's. I had chosen, once again—but it was obvious to Dad that I did not fear or avoid Daddy Jess, as I had himself. On perhaps the first of these early visits I forced myself to say the most difficult word ever to leave my mouth. It was the single syllable "Dad," in exchange for "Daddy," and I almost gagged on it. It implied so much more trust, respect, admiration, and desire for man-to-man companionship than the longer, child's word did—*and none of this did I feel.* Nevertheless, with the word "Dad" I let him, and myself, know I was a baby no more.

On another visit—a particularly untroubled one—I asked him to come upstairs with me. I had something to tell him and didn't want anyone else to hear. Hesitantly, I explained that boys' bodies held a fascination for me and that this worried me because I thought it was wrong. Oddly, his only replies—calm, at that—were that "Your mother once told me the most beautiful thing on earth, to her, was a man's body," and that I shouldn't worry, I would come to be interested in girls. He seemed glad, and surprised, that I'd confided in him. So was I—both.

Dad was entering his late forties, and I knew he was lonely. A year or two later—nine after my mother's death —he remarried. The event was to prove a blessing to both of us, and the beginning of a final and fulfilling reconciliation.

My father's new wife enforced a non-alcoholic regime, except for an occasional bottle of beer, on him. More importantly, she provided him with a happy and beautiful domesticity, something at which Mama had never been terribly adept. On my first visit to them in the small Ohio River town where they chose to live, I found, much to my surprise and joy, a mellowed, indulgent, and pleasant man in place of the angry and/or austere father I had known.

About twenty-one, and a man myself, I'd wondered whether I would still cringe a bit when a frown creased his face at some "unmanly" observation or gesture of mine, and whether conversation would be as awkward as ever. I spotted few, if any, frowns—and many unfamiliar (because they were new) grins. Conversation only faltered occasionally, for our lives and interests were now hundreds of miles apart.

The success of that first visit—and my obvious-to-Dad delight in the new wife—impelled me to see them more often. Eventually, when college was at an end, and career and the Good Gay Life had begun for me in the East, he himself made three one-week trips in as many summers— "to batch it with my son in the boy's New York apartment," he told the neighbors. On my own arrivals in Ohio, as well as on his in the East, we always greeted each other with a hug: arms around each other, and an almost-kiss, with sideburns rubbing. At first, when I initiated it, I had seen he would have been satisfied with less effusiveness. But I'd insisted on the hug. And he had grown to like it, and expect it too, and would have been disappointed and puzzled had it not been our opening gesture. Farewells claimed the same pleasant ritual.

Learning when he would arrive in New York, I got into the habit of leaving memos around, ostensibly to myself— "Fix drip in kitchen sink," "Rewire table lamp," etc.—and in some obvious spot. Dad knew I couldn't, or wouldn't, do these things. And, lo and behold! they would be done when I came home from work—he with a smile of satisfaction lighting his face. Well, he had to have *something* to do, didn't he, when he wasn't Circle Line'ing it or zooming to the top of the Empire State Building? Part of my motive for leaving the reminder notes around my studio was, in all honesty, that I knew he wanted to do something for me; I'd discovered how strong his desire was to make up for the lost years.

But what elated me most about his trips east was that, knowing I was "different," he—my once implacably All-American Butch Dad—nevertheless enjoyed being with me and made no bones about it.

Oh, I never told him about myself. I didn't need to. He'd had evidences enough of my sexual preference: an over-full personal telephone book with only three women's names in it, as one example. And, finally, I one day made the error of asking him to pick up my clean underclothing at the laundromat that afternoon. I had forgotten that under the last remaining pair of shorts and undershirt in my chest of drawers was my collection: pre-*Playgirl* photo-magazines of handsome (but miniclothed) muscle boys ranging as far back as early Reeves. When I returned from work, alarmed all day, I saw the clean underwear neatly arranged in the drawer. He must have found my cache! I gasped silently. But if he had noticed the crinkle of paper as he pressed the underclothes down one after another, and investigated, he gave no sign of it as he served up the beef bourguignon and string beans and wine that night. I have always wondered whether he believed I arranged that he should find out accidentally.

I must go back in time several years now, to a time when our rapprochement was rather new, and I must expand on an important character who triggered an immensely important event.

I have called her my grandmother up to this point, but must now present her, properly, as "Nana." In addition to more than making up for the loss of my mother, this gentle woman, another (but sleepier) movie companion and "buddy," about whom I could write a book, was the cause of the most emotionally charged and revealing moment of my relationship with my father.

It happened when she was dying.

A stroke had taken her speech and much of her movement shortly after Daddy Jess had passed away. I made an initial visit, back to Florida, then confided her to the care of a fine hospital and finer friends (including her sisters). I wrote every day, and soon planned to move her north to a rest home near me. This was the reason for Dad's, my stepmother's, and my joint trip south: to tell her, and make arrangements with the doctor.

After a week in the small Florida town, my father needed to get back to his job, and wanted to do so in a leisurely pattern, visiting parts of the South on his way home. The doctor, however, had told me that afternoon that Nana was suddenly "giving out," and that we might expect her to go into a coma and die in a matter of days. (Had she waited to see me this one last time before dying?)

That night, the three of us—Dad, my stepmother, and I—sat in the front seat of his automobile following our return from the hospital, and he repeated his desire to return north. I let him know what the doctor had told me: Could we wait a day or two longer? No, Dad replied. Though I could stay and travel back by train and he would give me extra cash if I was short of money.

At first, I was angry—for I well knew his dislike of my grandmother. Then my eyes began to water. "Dad," I started—and, surprised, I began to sob. "You . . . you always make me *choose* . . . choose between you and

N-Nana—just as you always made me ch-choose between you and Mama." I was quite visibly trembling by this time. "I'm not allowed . . . to . . . love . . . you . . . *both.* You . . . you won't let me. You never would." I put my hands up over my eyes. "I don't know what to do! D-don't make me choose. . . ."

My stepmother sat very still. But now I heard sobbing from the driver's seat. His words don't come back to me now—only the wrenching of his heart to the accompaniment of a choked and garbled response, the answer of a man touched by the knowledge—the final, real knowledge —that his son loves him.

Yes, we would stay two days more. But how insignificant his agreement seemed, next to the confessions we had just made to each other.

On one of my last crossings to Ohio before Dad himself died, he began with the usual small talk: "How was your trip across Pennsylvania?" and "Did you stop to visit your friends in Pittsburgh?" (He knew I had, but didn't know —?—that the "Pittsburgh friends" were a gay night on the town in the Golden Triangle city, with a peep into hustler-haunted Mellon Square.) It was Christmastime, and I had taken more than a week off. The Rose Bowl game was coming up, and, whatever else Dad may have sacrificed for me, his TV-sports afternoons were not on the list. The night before the game, with no hint of bitterness at what he'd long known was my lack of interest, but with a generous, even devilish, smile, he turned to my stepmother and me and said: "The game is on, tomorrow. Why don't you two go to a movie, if you like, or take the car and go for a drive, maybe go shopping? The game'll be over by 5:30." "You're sure you don't want company?" I inquired. "Nooo.

You don't enjoy this stuff, so go out and have some fun—away from the noise!" he said.

No immortal conversation. Nevertheless, to me it was the ultimate reassurance that he and I—multitudinously unalike as we were—had come to respect one another. And, yes, to love one another.

It had taken a long time. But it had come about. . . .

I have been a very lucky gay man. Not only did my progenitor make a successful effort to be what I had always deep-down wanted him to be, but I was myself ultimately able to see him as an oppressed and vulnerable human being, tied to many of society's misbegotten values and goals, and fully able to err. I, myself, erred for many years in blaming him for being a scornful and distant father, as well as for making me homosexual (the life has had its torments, though these are long past now).

I am glad that, on both scores, I've let Dad off the hook.

JIM GALLAGHER

My old man and I lived in two different worlds, on opposite sides of the American dream. As have so many fathers and sons who begin to drift apart, we spent a good many years shouting at one another, too many good years trying to bridge, with harsh words, an inevitable distance neither of us wanted and neither of us understood.

His was the world of his father, an Irish immigrant who worked on the railroad and belonged to the Knights of Columbus, a God-fearing man who taught his children to pay the bills on time and tend to their immortal souls. My father was a high school dropout, a toll collector who attended daily mass as often as possible and entertained his three children with stories from the Bible.

His favorite was the story of Lot's wife, who ignored God's command and looked behind her at the burning city of Sodom. For her curiosity, she was turned into a pillar of salt.

It was clear from the way he told it that he considered Lot's wife a fool, but I felt sorry for her. I knew in my heart I'd have done the same, and I marveled at Lot's ability to do what he was told. In my mind, I think, Lot and my father were one of the same.

I was his first-born son, but in an important sense I was never really his child. Something came between us early on —books, education, a bright new world of ideas he knew nothing about and was afraid of.

No doubt I caused him as much pain as he caused me; eventually he gave up—abandoned me to my own wiles, as he might have put it—and we became strangers to one another, living in the same house, eating at the same table, and suffering the same unspoken loneliness, not knowing how to approach one another, and avoiding each other to keep from trying.

Even today our relationship is a surface one, but I no longer think he's a stranger to me. I'm as old as he was when he first told me about Lot's wife, and I have three sons of my own, and I know that what I am, deep down, I am because he is what he is, and the things I like best about myself are not the things I learned in books but the things he gave me without either of us knowing—things I hope to pass on to my children.

On the morning my mother died, my father went to the hospital with my brother to collect her clothes, then disappeared for a few hours. None of us knew where he was, and we were concerned about him. When he finally came home, he explained something to me that put his whole life in perspective—mine, too.

When my mother was expecting my brother, he said, she became very ill with a kidney disease, and the doctors told my father she would more than likely die before the child was born. That afternoon, he went to church, and prayed in the very human way only those who truly believe can pray.

My mother never fully recovered, but she didn't die. She lived another twenty-five years with one kidney not functioning and the other damaged. When she finally died, my sister and I were married and my brother was engaged. On the morning she died, my father returned to that same church and said thank-you.

He was still a young man, and at that moment the future

must have looked empty and foreboding, but he already had been given more than he was entitled to, and this was a moment for gratitude, not bitterness.

Faith—that was the wall between us, his belief in a world order I could not accept. He wanted me to believe in his God, in his religion, in his values. What he never realized was that what you believe in is not as important as the fact that you do believe—in something other than your own flesh, something outside yourself that ennobles you, that forces you to adhere to standards, that makes you live up to your own humanity, and all the spirituality your humanity implies.

I could never bring myself to ask him, and he could never bring himself to tell me—we buried that part of us long before we buried my mother—but I sometimes wonder if he, too, doesn't secretly twinge at the grief we caused each other. If he does, I'd like to put his mind at ease. Whatever pain I felt has long since subsided; whatever wounds he inflicted have long since healed. I wish, somehow, he could say the same to me.

Funny, after all of this, the clearest memory I have of him is a happy one. I was about to leave the house on the morning of my first day in high school. I had to take a bus through a particularly bad neighborhood, then transfer to another one in a part of town I knew nothing about. Since no one I knew was going to the same school, I had to make the trek alone.

I was nervous, and my father sensed it. Perhaps he was nervous, too. He asked if I wanted company on the ride, and the casualness of my "yeah" belied the relief I was feeling. I don't remember if we said very much that morning—I don't suppose we did—but after that I took the trip for granted.

I can't recall ever telling my father I love him. I hope he takes it for granted. Because I do.

FREDERICK MANNING

That autumn, as the train swept southward over the yellowed, frostbitten land, I was racked with a kind of anxiety I had thought I'd forgotten how to feel. It had been only a light heart attack, he'd written—so light he hadn't wanted to worry us about it until he was up and about, all right again. Still, the sudden realization that anything *could* happen to my father (somehow I'd always thought of him as a permanent pillar of strength) filled me with a grave sense of urgency. As my wife Lisbeth, son Freddy and I rushed home to Alabama to see what the situation really was, my heart brimmed with a wordless eloquence—with all the love I had always felt for my father but had never been able to express.

This time, I told myself, I would *have* to find some right and proper way of telling him what he meant to me, to all of us.

Yet the moment we pulled into the station and saw him waiting on the platform, I began to get the self-conscious, almost tongue-tied feeling that comes when you experience an emotion too big for mere words.

Awkwardly we met and embraced, and I heard myself say, almost gruffly, "You sure you're really okay, Pop?"

"Fine," he said. "I'm feeling fine!"—though, with a sinking in the stomach, I could see that he wasn't fine at all. Despite his jauntiness, his youthful, invincible spirit that refused to grow old at seventy, he looked, at the moment, shaken, sick. His determination not to admit it, not to let us "worry" about it, brought a lump to my throat as he steered us toward the car.

There was an uncomfortable silence as we began the drive home. "Well, son," he asked after a while, "how's your work coming along?"

"Fine. And yours at the store?"

"Fine."

Then silence again, except for the swish of the tires on the pavement.

As we turned into the drive of our sprawling old family place, I felt a sharp pang of guilt. My four sisters and I had long since moved to different parts of the country, leaving Pop alone to cope with the big, now-too-quiet house and —since my mother's death—with his loneliness. The slight shagginess of the lawn gave me a keener stab. I thought of barefoot days when I'd kept the grass smooth-mown; of the extravagant compliments that Pop, coming home in the evenings, had had for my "work"; of long summer nights we'd sat together in the porch swing and planned what I'd do, what I'd be. I wanted to remind him, now, how much those talks meant to me.

But Pop, who must have seen something brewing in my eyes as we drove up to the door, said quickly, "Well, I guess we'd better get washed up for lunch."

The afternoon drifted away. Pop, Freddy and I took a little walk down by the creek where Pop and I used to spend so many hours. We talked about fishing, mostly.

That night Lisbeth and Freddy went to bed early. Pop and I were sitting out on the porch swing, listening to the rusty chains creak slowly, watching the passing lights of cars, which made the shadows of the gingerbread banisters march in curious procession along the walls. A little to the left of the willow tree, now grown tall, thick and unfamiliar, a harvest moon was rising. "When the moon reaches the tree," I thought, "I'll start trying to say it."

It wasn't the things he had done without in order to provide for his family that I loved him for. It was the experiences we had shared.

"Pop," I wanted to say, "do you know what the world was like when I was seven—Freddy's age? Well, it was a place where, when you were around—even asleep in the next room—everything was all right. There was nothing to be afraid of, not even these shadows of banisters marching across the porch. I thought the world was in good, safe hands because there were people like you up there somewhere running things."

I wanted to bring up times that were as far away now as knee-length bathing suits; or cooling watermelons in a cold creek hole on the Fourth of July; or catching lightning bugs at dusk and putting them in milk bottles to show him; or pitching ball with him on some long, school-less, midsummer afternoon.

But most of all I wanted to tell Pop about the special day. "Tell him at least about that," I ordered myself, as the moon edged toward the shaggy willow. Wouldn't it mean something to him to know how well I remembered that special day thirty years ago?

That morning it had still been dark when I awoke to the unusual sound of Pop making a fire in the grate in my bedroom. When I sat up, rubbing my eyes, the room was full of dancing yellow light and the good, warm smell of newspapers and fat pine burning.

He had a lot of nonsensical names he called me then.

"Well, Old Timer," he'd say, or "Well, Old Snickel-fritz . . ." With names like that alone he could start creating the special, lighthearted world he thought that all children were entitled to.

"Well, Old Timer," he called out that morning, "rise and shine! We're going hunting together today—just you and I." Pop always had the knack of communicating high excitement about things to come, but that morning of my first hunt he outdid himself.

"Up and at 'em," he said. "We're going to have quite a day, quite a day. I'm cooking us some sausage. It's something that'll stay with a man."

The sausage was burned—it always was when Pop cooked it—and the eggs were brown and greasy. But after that, burned sausage and eggs cooked too brown always summoned up the anticipation of adventure.

"Well, Pop," I wanted to say to the seventy-year-old man in the swing beside me now, "it wasn't much of a hunt, as hunts go—nothing to compare with some of the hunts we had later. But it was the day that seemed to start it all, our closeness, our sharing of things good and bad together. Funny thing, Pop, but after that the smell of a hunting coat always smelled to me like strength and security—the way you smelled standing there that morning warming up the room for me."

Well, a man pushing forty just can't say things like that, not out loud. The moon reached the top of the willow and went on across it, and I still sat dumbly.

"Chilly tonight," Pop said finally. "Fallish. Be cold in the morning."

"I guess so," I said.

We lapsed into small talk again, and went to bed.

By the fifth night—we were leaving two days later—the silences between Pop and me had lengthened even more. I gave up the idea of ever trying to get my thoughts across to him. The whole attempt, I decided, had been mawkish.

It occurred to me, too, that I'd been neglecting my own son. The week hadn't been much fun for him. Suddenly, I wanted to show Freddy that this wasn't just a ghost of a house, to hint to him something of the bright, warm times I'd known here.

It was cold and dark when the clock went off at four the next morning. I shivered as I tiptoed into my old room—the one where Freddy was sleeping—and built a fire. The yellow pine was crackling merrily, washing the room in warm, gay light, when I shook him awake.

"Get up, Old Timer," I said to him. "We're going hunting together, you and I." I could see by the way he began jumping into his clothes that my voice carried the proper excitement. "We're going to have quite a time together."

I was burning the sausage and, despite all I could do, getting the eggs too brown when I turned and saw Pop standing in the kitchen doorway. As he stood, nightgown-clad, I saw it slowly dawn on him that he was looking in on an old and familiar scene, an act from a favorite play of ours of long ago.

His eyes questioned at first, then comprehended. In one quick glance Pop saw how faithfully I was trying to do for my son exactly the things he'd done for me, how I was hoping to pass on to Freddy something of the same magic he had made me feel. I'm certain that he realized, too, that not just one good day but a lifetime of good days was beginning all over again—or continuing.

Gruffly, to hide his emotion, Pop said, "What in heav-

en's name are you two doing up in the middle of the night?
And why haven't you ever learned to cook?"

But from the way he looked at Freddy and me as we
started out into the early light together in the old hunting
coats, I knew he understood—understood all the volumes
of difficult things I need not ever again try to say.

Even before he put a hand on each of our shoulders and
said, "Well, good luck, Old Timers," I knew that, without
speaking, I had told him that I loved him. And I knew that
he had heard me.

JOHN ED BRADLEY

The last time my father and I did anything together, we were out playing eighteen holes of golf at the Indian Hills Country Club, and, seeing him in the sun, I couldn't get over the peppery gray that highlighted what only a few years before had been a bristly blond mustache. He was . . . still the most handsome man I knew, still the best.

"You're getting old, Pip," I said as he prepared to clobber a ball with his expensive graphite club. I was trying to wreck his concentration so he'd muff the shot. And he knew it. He looked up from the tee and his eyes blazed, and he smiled the most extraordinary smile. He swiveled his hips the way he'd seen the pros do on television, and he reset his spiked shoes.

"Just don't blow it," I said. "We've already lost six balls."

"Yeah, but you lost five of 'em."

"Please don't make it seven," I said.

He pulled back and readied to swing, and for some unknown reason I said, "I love you, Pip. You know I love you, don't you?"

But he was quiet, fixed in concentration, watching the ball sail off to the right, deep in the tall pine trees.

GEORGE EYRE MASTERS

It was a typical June day in San Francisco, cool and over-cast. Reading the newspaper I noticed the East Coast was suffering a heat wave and Father's Day was approaching. Father's Day, like Mother's Day, never meant much to me. I've generally regarded those days as good for merchants and convenient for children.

Putting down the paper I looked up at a photograph of Father on my desk. My sister had taken it several summers ago in Biddeford Pool, Maine. Father and I stood together on the porch of a cottage, our arms around each other's shoulders. By the looks of us the apple didn't fall far from the tree. Father's Day, I mused, and thought about calling to see how he and Mother were doing.

Picking up the photograph I examined it closely. That was my old man, no doubt about it. With his top teeth out, he grinned like a grizzled ex-hockey player. His eyes were set deep in a sun-creased face with a cocky stance at seventy years old. I could smell his Lucky Strikes, scotch and bay rum.

It was a younger man who used to chase me along the beach and take me into the water, a stronger man who taught me how to row, skate and split firewood. That was before his plastic knee, false teeth and hearing aid. I decided to give the old man a call.

"Good afternoon," he shouted. Mother picked up the other phone and told him to put his hearing aid in.

"I've got it here in my pocket," he said, and I heard him fumbling for it.

Mother said the air conditioning was a godsend, her plastic hip was all right and the new dog was driving her nuts.

"Actually," she said, "it's not the dog, it's your father."

"What's the matter?" I asked.

"Shep can jump over the fence and does whenever the mood strikes him, then takes off into God knows where. Your father worries about Shep and waits up until he comes back. He's out there at two in the morning, calling the dog and making an awful racket. Then when Shep comes back, he scolds him, 'Malo perro, malo, malo,' as if we were back in Peru and the dog understands Spanish."

"I think he's learning," said Father, back on the line. "Your mother thinks I'm a damn fool and she's probably right."

"You're still shouting," said Mother.

He ignored her and asked me how I was doing. I told him.

"Free-lancing is fine," he said loudly, "but you need security. You're too old to be cooking on yachts, tending bar and working construction. You've got a college education, why don't you use it? What are you going to do if you get sick? You know how much it costs to stay in a hospital?"

"You know," I told him, "I can't figure you out. You smoke too much, drink too much, don't exercise and you eat all the wrong foods and still you're a tough old goat."

"You're right," he said. "And I'm outliving all my classmates." He said it without bragging.

There was something I wanted to tell the old man and I was having a difficult time getting it out.

"Do you read the newspaper clippings I send you?" he asked.

"Sure, I do."

"I don't know whether you do or not, you never write."

I wasn't forgetting that he and I had had our differences over the past forty-four years and that we had angered, disappointed and cursed each other often. But those times seemed long ago and I wanted to tell him I loved him. I wanted to be funny and I wanted the telephone call to flow.

"Listen," I told him, "I understand Father's Day is coming up."

"Oh?" he said, uninterested. He never kept track.

"It's the seventeenth," said Mother on the other phone.

"I'm sorry I jumped through the top of your Lincoln convertible," I said.

"You were six," he said and chuckled. "I couldn't believe it at first."

I wanted to thank him for the hockey games, chess games, books and lobster dinners. I wanted to apologize for punching him in the eye when I was eighteen.

"Thanks for being my father," I said.

He was quiet on his end and Mother was too. A long-distance micro static filled the void.

"I wish I'd been better," he said, his voice subdued for the first time.

"You were just fine," I said. "A guy couldn't have had a better father."

"Good of you to say, old boy, but not true. I wish it were," he said with regret in his voice.

"It is true," I said and hurried on, "Do you remember when I wanted to feed sugar to the donkey at the Cricket Club and you patted him on the rump and he kicked you?"

"Yes," chuckled Father. "Smashed my knee, damn beast. You always thought that was funny."

"And all those ships you took me aboard," I added.

"There were a few of those," he conceded. "Boy, you're really taking me back."

"I loved the ships," I told him.

"But still I couldn't convince you to go in the Navy."

"I wanted you to go to college after high school," said Mother.

"But you wouldn't listen," said Father. "You had to be a Marine."

I didn't say anything. I heard them remembering.

"And we flew out to California," continued Father, "to say good-bye before you left for Vietnam."

"We stayed at the Newporter Inn," said Mother, "and went to Disneyland."

Father continued, "I had to leave that Sunday night by helicopter to catch a flight out of Los Angeles. Your mother and the girls stayed in the hotel and you walked me to the helipad. You were in uniform and we shook hands. . . ." His voice trailed off. "It Tore Me Up.

"I didn't know if I'd ever see you again," he said. "I cried on that helicopter. It tore me up, your leaving."

"I know," I said and felt a lump in my throat.

"We prayed for you," he said, his voice beginning to tremble. "We lived for your letters."

"And I for yours," I told him. This was crazy, I thought. My eyes were damp and I swallowed to clear the lump.

"I called to wish you a happy Father's Day," I managed.

"That was good of you, old boy. I'll hang up now, don't want to run up your bill." His voice was shaking.

"Don't worry about the bill," I said, "I love you."

"I love you too. Good-bye and God bless you," he said hurriedly and hung up.

"You know how he gets," said Mother quietly on the other phone.

"I know," I said, and after another minute we said good-bye and hung up.

I looked at the photograph of Father and me on the porch in Maine. Yes, I thought, I know how he gets. I wiped my eyes, smiled at the picture and blew my nose loudly. The apple didn't fall far from the tree.

6

Requiem

JOEL GREY / RONALD KOERTGE

DAVID WOJAHN / PHILIP B. KUNHARDT, JR.

DAVID PLANTE / ANATOLE BROYARD

ROBERT BLY / ALASTAIR REID

JAMES DICKEY / ROBERT ALAN AURTHUR

LEWIS GRIZZARD / JAMES A. CUNNINGHAM

ANDREW H. MALCOLM / ERIC LAX

BURT PRELUTSKY

JOEL GREY

I'm remembering a time a number of years ago when my father was quite ill . . . and the tone in my brother's voice as he said it would be a good idea if I were to fly to Los Angeles as soon as possible. My wife and I were on the next plane, and I found myself filled with the strange and reflective melancholy that seems so often to accompany events of impending life-altering importance—births, deaths, long-term commitments.

We were standing at his hospital bed and when he realized we were there, he said to me, "I forgot to pick you up." He was weeping. "I'm sorry." I was confused until I realized that he was delirious and reliving a painful past experience. It seems I was six or seven years old. He was to pick me up at school, as always, but on this particular day his watch might have been incorrect, or he miscalculated the time—it makes no difference—the point is that I waited and waited at school and then walked home by myself. Naturally, I was confused and perhaps a bit frightened, but hardly scarred or traumatized; yet he took his responsibility so seriously, he cared so much, that even then, twenty-five years later, it remained in his thoughts.

RONALD KOERTGE

MY FATHER

Lies on the same couch that he used to
only sit on, straight up as if the newsmen
might ask him to spring into action.

He used to work twelve hours a day making
ice cream from scratch. Then home, charging
around the lawn. Grass that had been mashed
flat he brought to attention then cut it off
at the roots, snuffing it out,
heartless.

He took one vacation, looking at the water in
Michigan with one eye, turning at every little
thing, each sound a customer. We dined at
roadside stands, covering six states in a week.
He ate standing, like a man on the run.

I saw him again last summer, four months past a
coronary. He rested in bed, gathering strength
for a nap, hands behind his head,
eyes full of ceilings.

DAVID WOJAHN

HEAVEN FOR RAILROAD MEN

You're still a young man,
he says, not to his son;
it's his bitterness
he's talking to
and at the restaurant
he orders a fourth round
before dinner,
with mother wiping her glasses
at the table, still believing
she's not going blind.

I help him from his chair
to the john. He pees slowly,
fingers like hams
on his fly, a complex
test of logic
for a man this drunk.
I'm splashing cold water on his face

and he tells me he's dying,
don't say a thing to your
mother and please, Dave,
don't ever remember me like this.

I remember how you said you
needed to
ride the baggage cars forever,
passing prairie towns

where silos squat like
pepper shakers on dry earth.
Father, I want to be six again
and sway with you

down the sagging rails
to Minot, Winnipeg, and beyond,
your mailsacks piled
like foothills of the Rockies.
You're unloading your government Colt,
unzipping your suitcase
for Canadian inspectors.
Father, when I touched you
I was trembling.

The heaven
of railroad men begins
with a collapsed trestle.
The engine goes steaming off
into nothing.
There are no rails to hold you,
you're singing country western
at the top of your lungs,
you go flying forever,
the door standing open,
sacks of mail scattering
like seed into space.

PHILIP B. KUNHARDT, JR.

In the late autumn of 1962 my father was in his upstairs bed at home. When one of us called to say we were coming to visit, he would struggle up, get somehow to the top of the stairs, sit on the top step holding the banister, then edge himself down each stair, one by one—it would take him half an hour to make the trip—so that he would be in his chair in the living room to greet us with a smile when we arrived.

Once, toward winter, I worked late in the city and then drove out unannounced after midnight to the hill. I found the front door locked, climbed through a window and lay down on a couch in the living room so that I could be there in the morning for a visit with him. Except for me, only my mother and father were in the house, and all night long I heard her getting up at his call, tending him. "Oh, my love. That's it, my sweet boy. It's all right, dearest. You're my sweet husband. My love."

I could not bear to hear it, could not help, could not intrude. I lay there on the couch all night without sleeping, trying to come to terms with the knowledge my father was really and truly dying. I would probably see him only a few times more. I wondered what there was to say between us that had not been said. Was there anything that I should know from him or anything that he should know from me? . . .

The next morning when I went upstairs to see him he was trying to hobble his way into the bathroom. He went slowly, grabbing onto pieces of furniture for balance, fighting the pain in his leg and through his body, fighting in the same way he had fought through football practice and games forty years before. "Come on, Kunhardt," I overheard him calling himself by his last name just as his coach had done it back in college. "Let's go now. Don't give up! You mustn't! Get on with you! Go!"

DAVID PLANTE

FROM *THE COUNTRY*

I went into the living room which, too, was dim. My father was sitting straight upright in a big wing chair, hands folded on his lap, his eyes wide open; he stared at me as I came towards him, his mouth a little open, but he said nothing. His plaid woollen shirt was unbuttoned, showing his undershirt.

I said, "Père."

My father's breath was wheezing. The lid of one of his eyes was turned in, and rimmed with yellow matter.

"I thought I'd come to find out how you are."

In a very short breath, just long enough for him to expel the words, my father said, "I'm all right."

"Père," I said louder.

My father tapped his chest. "I can't talk."

"You should try."

He kept his hand on his chest. He looked down at his shirt and after a moment he tried to button the buttons, but he did not seem able to bend his fingers.

Looking up at me, he said, "Will you button my shirt?"

I stepped away from him as to step away from his body.

"Will you?" he asked.

I crossed my arms at my waist. "You can't do it?"

"No."

I could not touch my father's body. "It doesn't matter, does it, that it's left unbuttoned?"

My father lowered his hands to his lap.

I held myself more closely about my waist and sat on a chair next to my father and watched him.

My father looked out into the dim room, his face stark, and while he looked out he picked at his thumbnail with the nails of his other hand. As if he had been unaware, then was suddenly aware of someone by him, he turned his head to me.

After a long while, I asked, "What is it?"

He said, "The nail of my thumb is broken."

"You can't cut it?"

"I can't, no."

"Let me see," I said, and took his hand. The nails were yellow and long and some of them were cracked. I said, "I'll cut them for you."

My father didn't answer.

In the medicine cabinet over the bathroom washbasin I found a clipper and nail scissors. I took a towel, too, which I placed over my father's knees. He held out one hand, and I grasped it at the wrist, and I clipped the nails. One hand finished, I placed it on my father's knee, and he raised the other to me.

I asked, "What about your toenails?"

My father, as if stunned, said nothing.

"I'll cut your toenails."

"I'll have to wash my feet."

"No, don't worry about that," I said, and I bent further over to untie my father's shoes as he lifted each foot in turn. I pulled off his shoes and drew down his socks. The narrow feet were very white; the toes were twisted. I spread the towel under them. I took the sole of his right foot in my palm and turned round to hold his foot under my arm so I could cut the nails with the scissors; it was like cutting horn.

I blinked to rid my eyes of tears.

When I finished I put my father's socks back on, and his shoes, which I tied.

I asked, "Is there anything else you want me to do for you?"

"No, sir," my father said.

I stood for a while before him. I said, "Père."

"Yes."

I frowned. "You know who I am, don't you?"

"Yes, you're my son Daniel."

"You mustn't say sir to me. I should say sir to you. You're my father.". . .

He raised his head; his eyes were brimming. He said to me, "I've been a bad man."

I stood and leaned over him. He was not able to shave properly, and under his chin and on his neck were patches of long white hairs. His eyes over-brimmed. The one with the infolded lid was half closed. With a little moan, as if to expel enough breath to speak, he said, "I have."

I held my father; I pressed the side of his face against my face.

My father said, with many long breathless pauses, "I have done no good, none to your mother, none to you boys."

"Père," I said.

"I have done no good in the world."

"Père, Père, you have worked so hard."

"For no good."

I rocked him back and forth in my arms as he wept

against the side of my face. He then kissed me, on my neck, just below my ear. I held him more tightly.

When I drew back I saw my father's contorted face. He reached into his trouser pocket for his handkerchief, wiped his eyes and cheeks.

ANATOLE BROYARD

When I was a boy, my father's silence was one of the great mysteries of my life. Not only did he fail to answer when I spoke to him, he didn't even seem to hear me. There was no sign, no flicker in his face, to show that I had spoken and I sometimes wondered whether I actually had. I used to stand there and listen, trying to catch the echo of my voice.

If I could have got my father's eye, could have looked him squarely in the face, I might have compelled him to answer me, or at least to acknowledge that I had spoken, but it was impossible to do this because he had a way of turning his head to one side, like a horse. I would walk around him, like someone circling a statue in a museum. Just as in medieval paintings people hold their heads to one side, so in my memory my father's face is always turned.

There came a time at last when he couldn't look away. He was in a hospital bed and it would have been too painful to turn his head because the illness had spread to his bones. When I placed myself in his line of sight, he had to see me.

It was our last chance to talk and I felt all that I had to say thrilling along my nerves. I had a lifetime of small and large talk saved up. I took a great breath, opened my mouth like an opera singer, but only a sigh came out, because talk doesn't keep. Everything was concreted into lumps, like stuff left too long in the refrigerator. At the very end, I told my father that I would miss him. I did not say that I had always missed him.

ROBERT BLY

MY FATHER AT EIGHTY-FIVE

His large ears
hear everything.
A hermit wakes
and sleeps in a hut
underneath
his gaunt cheeks.
His eyes blue,
alert, dis-
appointed and suspicious
complain
I do not bring him
the same sort of jokes
the nurses do. He
is a small bird
waiting to be fed,
mostly beak,
and eagle, or a vulture, or
the Pharoah's servant
just before death.
My arm on the bedrail
rests there, relaxed,
with new love.
All I know of the Troubadours
I bring
to this bed.
I do not want
or need

to be shamed
by him
any longer.
The general of shame
has discharged
him and left him in this
small provincial
Egyptian town.
If I do not wish
to shame him, then
why not
love him?
His long hands,
large, veined, capable,
can still retain
hold of what
he wanted.
But is that
what he desired?
Some powerful
river of desire
goes on flowing
through him.
He never phrased
what he desired,
and I am
his son.

ALASTAIR REID

MY FATHER, DYING

At summer's succulent end,
the house is green-stained.
I reach for my father's hand

and study his ancient nails.
Feeble-bodied, yet at intervals
a sweetness appears and prevails.

The heavy-scented night
seems to get at his throat.
It is as if the dark coughed.

In the other rooms of the house,
the furniture stands mumchance.
Age has graved his face.

Cradling his wagged-out chin,
I shave him, feeling bone
stretching the waxed skin.

By his bed, the newspaper lies furled.
He has grown too old
to unfold the world

which has dwindled to the size of a sheet.
His room has a stillness to it.
I do not call it waiting, but I wait,

anxious in the dark, to see if
the butterfly of his breath
has fluttered clear of death.

There is so much might be said,
dear old man, before I find you dead;
but we have become too separate

now in human time
to unravel all the interim
as your memory goes numb.

But there is no need for you to tell—
no words, no wise counsel,
no talk of dying well.

We have become mostly hands
and voices in your understanding.
The whole household is pending.

I am not ready
to be without your frail and wasted body,
your miscellaneous mind-way,

the faltering vein of your life.
Each evening, I am loath
to leave you to your death.

Nor will I dwell on
the endless, cumulative question
I ask, being your son.

But on any one
of these nights soon,
for you, the dark will not crack with dawn,

and then I will begin
with you that hesitant conversation
going on and on and on.

JAMES DICKEY

Long deathwatch with my father. Nothing in his wasted and lovable life has ever become him so much as when he moved close to death. It is astonishing to understand that one's father is a brave man: very brave. The only thing he worried about was my seeing him in that condition. He cannot ever understand, whether he lives or whether he dies, how much better he looked with his arms full of tubes, with one of those plastic hospital things in his nose, and the rest of it, than at any time I have ever seen him before. He was a man up against an absolute limit, and he was giving as well as he got and he was afraid of nothing in this world or out of it. God bless that man. No matter how I came from him, I hope that it was in joy. For the end is courage.

ROBERT ALAN AURTHUR

From the time last March when I flew with my father to Florida, there to leave him, sick and helpless, in a nursing home, eight months passed before he died. He went very hard, at the peak of a rage that devastated everyone around him, his anger fueled not by the fact of death, which I think he understood as well as anyone can, but by the sure knowledge of its imminence. The final cause was said to be lung cancer, but there had been other crippling complications to plague him for nearly two years. At seventy-one he had been a robust one-hundred-eighty pounds, working a full day, with enough energy to give away. At seventy-three, a monument of sorts to over a million cigarettes and countless quarts of Canadian whisky, weighing less than a hundred pounds, he died.

Now I'll tell you the worst part: when he died I was glad. Whatever the balance of love and hostility that existed between us over a lifetime, most of his and all of mine, at the end there was only hostility. He hated me. *I* had put him in this place to die, and *I* could change nothing. And, for me, at the very end there was no one to love. This skeletal being, this pitiful creature whose only sentient moments were used for hammer blows against me, his worst and only enemy, was not my father. What we experienced at the end was new, different—unrelated to any of the total experience we had together in life; this unique horror had only to do with death. During each of the four trips I made to see my father, there would come that moment when he would say to me, "Get me out of here. I don't want to die here." And I would say, "Tell me where you do want to die, I'll take you there." Then, a cruel moment of silence before my father would talk of something else, like how much he hated palm trees. Oh, yes, the process of dying creates its own little rituals, every one of them based in absolute hopelessness. . . .

. . . I think my father's anger stemmed mostly from his realization, easily measured, that day by day he was becoming less than human. Here was a man who, like other American fathers, taught his kid to play baseball, at his best could toss a perfectly spiraling football to a mark forty yards away, was always known as a hell of a dancer, and during the Twenties even had a shot at being a film actor. Now, at age seventy-three, he lay in a bed, unable to control body functions, forced at times to lie in his own excrement, until kindly strangers came to clean him. Unable to eat without choking and spitting up, like some kind of gaunt, grotesque infant, a good day was one when he would be strapped into a wheelchair and pushed onto a veranda. To see what?—a dusty road, the hospital across the way, and the palm trees he professed to hate. . . .

. . . Is it enough simply to remember the past, knowing there is no future? I once asked my father, and he said, "The worst thing is the discovery that boredom is actively painful. It hurts!" Then, why cling to a life where the ultimate, the *only* pleasures, are a wheelchair ride down a hallway, a five-hour stretch of sleep without nightmare?

And here's another part of the horror, the moment when you become your father's own executioner, for what is an executioner but someone who cuts another's life short? Never mind whether it's years or days, the executioner takes time away.

I stand in my father's room. He's in a semicoma, doesn't know me, yet he shouts out names from the past, among them mine. He calls me Bobby, a name I've not heard since I was five. Breathing is an agony, yet he doesn't want to die. I go to a phone, call his doctor, who has ultramodern space in the newest building in the area; he's a pleasant, serious, caring man, younger than I am. This young man and I have been leveling with one another from the beginning of an entirely formal relationship. He's custodian of my father's death, but I make the decisions. He calls me Mister and says Sir, and I sometimes get the feeling he's afraid of me. He doesn't want to get blamed for anything. On the phone I say, "It's very bad, isn't it," and he says, "Yes, it is." I ask how long, and he estimates two weeks, a month. Then he says, "An additional problem now is that he's unable to take much nourishment. We could prolong the situation by special feeding." I ask how much longer that would add to my father's life, and he hesitantly suggests something like a week or two, then says, "But we really don't know." The decision is mine.

And so, in the end, with a promise from the doctor that every effort will be made to hold off pain, I take away some of my father's life. What a dismal curtain to the universal Freudian drama, to be handed the actual weapon. Yet, in such a civilized, acceptable arena, who will ever accuse me, much less bring me to justice? . . .

The last physical act I ever did for my father was that day when I held a cigarette to his lips and watched him mindlessly suck a half-dozen puffs of smoke until too racked by coughs to take another drag. I stub out the butt and turn to leave, coming face-to-face with a mirror. There I see a reflection of my father as I remember him nearly twenty-five years ago. I resolve not to look in a mirror for a while, and on the way to the airport I smoke two cigarettes.

LEWIS GRIZZARD

My father was living in this little town down near Savannah. He'd had a stroke on the street and after he was in the hospital a few days he got pneumonia. I was living in Atlanta and I'd been down to see him about three days earlier. He was unconscious then and was having these awful convulsions. I don't think he knew I was there.

I finally had to leave him and come back home to work. But one morning I get this phone call at about four and a nurse at the hospital tells me things are pretty bad and if I want to see him one more time while he's alive, I'd better come in a hurry.

It was over a four-hour drive down there, but I made it a lot faster. I kept praying the whole time I was driving that this whole thing was some kind of nightmare and I'd wake up.

I got to the hospital and they showed me where his room was. There were three other men in the room, men from his church. Daddy loved going to church. It's how he made friends. He would go into a church in some little town where he was going to live for a while and he'd sit right down front so everybody could see him.

He had a beautiful baritone voice, and when the singing would start, he would belt it out as loudly and as forcefully as he could. After the services everyone would want to meet the handsome, gray-haired man with the beautiful voice.

I shook hands with the three men after I walked into the room. . . .

I looked down at him on the bed. He was a big, stout man. He'd been through two wars and all sorts of other hells, and he looked pitiful lying there in that bed. And he was blue. I swear to God he was blue.

I took his right hand. It was cold. I pressed it tightly with my hands. He didn't respond. He was breathing so slowly. One breath, and then when you didn't think he would breathe again, he would gasp for one more.

I had never seen anybody die before. I didn't know what in hell to expect. I imagined there would be doctors and nurses all around a dying man, trying to save him. There weren't. There wasn't anybody but me and three men from the church.

I asked had a doctor been in. One of the men said his doctor had come by a little earlier, but said there wasn't anything he or anybody else could do.

I really didn't know how I was supposed to act. I was twenty-three, I guess, old enough not to want to carry on in front of a roomful of other men. So I didn't cry. I even thought that maybe his dying wasn't that awful a thing. When one of his brothers, my uncle, heard he was in bad shape, he'd even thought the same thing. "He's been through enough hell as it is," is what my uncle said.

God, how I had to agree with that. There were the two wars, and when he came home from Korea, he was totally messed up. Couldn't sleep. Couldn't stay off the phone. He'd get so drunk and then get on the phone. He'd cry. Lord, he'd cry. I remember my mama fighting with him over the big telephone bills.

He started borrowing money, too. Lots of it. And nobody could figure out why. Mother would say, "Lewis, where is all that money going?" . . .

I was still holding his hand when he took his last breath. He breathed and then he didn't breathe again. It seemed like a peaceful death. I don't think he was in any pain. I wanted to talk to him, to tell him how much I loved him, but it was better he go that way.

One of the men from the church went and got a nurse. She felt for a pulse but didn't find one. Without a word, she went out of the room, then came back with a doctor. The doctor put his stethoscope on Daddy's chest and listened. I was still holding his hand, when the doctor looked at me and said, "He's gone."

I let go of his hand. The nurse pulled the sheet over his head and then went out of the room behind the doctor. One of the three men said we ought to pray, and so he said a prayer. I don't remember which one, though.

I was in a daze.

I called my mother. She said she was sorry. I knew she was, both for me and for her. My daddy was not the kind of man you could stop loving, no matter what he did to you.

Then I called my uncle and he said he'd make some arrangements about bringing the body back to Atlanta, about the funeral. After I hung up, I had no idea what to do next.

There was the hospital bill. It was eight hundred dollars. Daddy didn't have any insurance. I didn't have eight hundred dollars. A good friend helped me pay it. They had said they wouldn't let the body go until I paid the bill. A woman said it was hospital policy to get this sort of thing cleared up as quickly as possible.

All Daddy had was in one of those plastic garbage bags. I remember opening the bag and going through his belongings. There were the clothes he had worn into the hospital. There was a ring. It didn't look like it was worth much. His old watch was in the bag, and so was his wallet. There was nothing in the wallet, no money, not a single piece of identification. I looked inside his coat and found a letter he had been carrying.

It was a letter from me. I had written it six months before. It was short, maybe a page, typewritten. Down at the end, I had given him some grief about straightening out his life. I told him I would have to think twice about inviting him to my house again if he didn't promise he wouldn't show up drinking. I'd just signed my name. I didn't say "love" or anything. I had just signed my goddamned name like I was a real hardass.

I still wonder why he carried such a letter around with him for so long. Maybe he kept it as a reminder to do better. I don't know. Maybe he kept it to remind himself his only son was turning on him. Whatever, I never forgave myself for that letter. I can't get it out of my head he died not knowing how much I loved him.

JAMES A. CUNNINGHAM

My medical suite was designed for two doctors, and I moved in with the idea of eventually adding a junior partner. I never dreamed that five years later the person occupying the other office would be my seventy-nine-year-old terminally ill father. But it happened, and it was one of the most valuable experiences of my life.

The idea came to me late last April while I was driving home after a long, trying day. I'd worked my usual morning office hours, made my rounds, and driven 150 miles to Cadiz, Ky., and back, to see my hospitalized father. He'd been confined for five weeks and was barely holding on. In the corridor, my sister had whispered: "This is it, isn't it? He's not going to make it home." . . .

Dad had never been hospitalized before, and now he proclaimed: "I'm not going to die in a hospital, or a bed or a rocking chair at home. When I die, it'll be on a dance floor."

He never made much money, but he loved people. He particularly liked to organize and attend dances at various senior citizens' centers in the area. He'd often drive fifty miles or more to these events, sometimes four or five days a week. My mother, who was less outgoing than Dad, never went along; she preferred the Homemakers Club and her church activities.

Late one night, my mother received a call from the state police: They'd found Dad's car burning on Interstate 24 about twenty miles from home. She thought he'd burned to death, and was about to notify the rest of us when Dad walked in the back door. He matter-of-factly explained that his car had caught fire, so he'd hitched a ride home.

In March 1985, his penile carcinoma worsened and he had to consent to be hospitalized for the amputation. He quickly recovered and returned to his old ways. Once a month, he'd drive the 150 miles from Cadiz to my office for a checkup, stay the weekend, then return home to resume his busy schedule with the senior citizens. He particularly enjoyed houseboating with us that summer—swimming, and paddling in my kayak for hours.

With his vigor and his full head of still-not-gray hair, Dad didn't look his age, and he told almost no one of his terminal illness. It was still in remission in September 1985, when he was commissioned a Kentucky colonel in honor of his efforts for senior citizens.

On Christmas Day, 1985, we took him and the whole family to a Chinese restaurant for dinner—his first time for Chinese food. It was a joyous occasion, but I had the feeling it might be our last big get-together—that Dad wouldn't make it until June 2, 1986, his eightieth birthday.

The end began in March 1986. I found hematuria on routine urinalysis, and cystoscopy confirmed that the tumor had invaded his bladder. His spleen had grown to gigantic size and was causing him considerable suffering. He rarely complained, however, and refused pain medication. Although he was told that the pain from his spleen would worsen and the tumor would soon obstruct his urine flow, he refused palliative surgery. We knew it was only a matter of time before he'd need hospitalization for antibiotics or a blood transfusion.

Dad was admitted to the hospital in Cadiz on March 26 with an infected right foot. When it had to be amputated, he nearly lost his will to live. He knew he'd never dance or drive again. To make things worse, the bladder tumor was now obstructing his urethra completely, and a suprapubic catheter had to be inserted. In addition, he was losing blood rapidly through the urinary tract, and he had to have multiple transfusions over the next five weeks. The blood loss drained him of almost all strength, and he could talk only for short periods.

When I arrived at the hospital that April day, he told me: "There are too many complications. I've made my peace, and I'm ready to go." Then he began to cry like a child, as he begged to go home: "I don't want to die in this hospital." We watched a baseball game on TV that night, then he cried once more as I left. He was afraid he'd never see me again.

As I drove home, I tried to figure out some way to grant Dad's wish. My mother, who had health problems of her own, couldn't manage his care at home even with daily nursing assistance. My sister, Elaine, was a teacher, and had neither the time, facilities, nor know-how. This left my house, with an inconvenient upstairs guest room and a downstairs awkwardly arranged for someone in a wheelchair. Despite this, Nancy, my wife and office manager, would gladly have nursed him at home—but he was my father, my responsibility.

Then it occurred to me—I'd move him into the vacant office planned for a second doctor. It was large and could easily be made into a temporary hospital room. Our staff could help during the day, and Nancy and I could take turns sleeping in the extra exam room at night. The office even had a refrigerator, hot plate, and toaster oven.

Nancy and the rest of the office staff were pleased and

eager to help when I told them my plans the next day. The first thing was to call Dad and give him hope. There was immediate optimism in his voice when I told him. We discussed transportation, and he said he didn't want an ambulance. I suggested renting a station wagon "from Hertz." No, he said, he didn't want a hearse either, and we had a big laugh.

Next we called an equipment company and arranged for a hospital bed and commode chair to be delivered to my office. We already had a wheelchair. My seventeen-year-old son, Paul, contributed his small TV set so his granddaddy could watch baseball games and cheer for his favorite St. Louis Cardinals. I borrowed a custom van, and Nancy and I were off to Cadiz to collect the patient.

The van had a bed, and the seats reclined. But Dad was so excited he sat up for the entire three-hour drive. He'd often made this trip on his own; now he enjoyed every mile as a passenger. When we arrived at the office, he was tired but ecstatic. "You don't know how much it means to me for you and Nancy to be doing this," he said. We moved him into his new room and fed him supper. Off he went into a contented sleep.

The next morning, he asked to eat breakfast at the table in our lab. Later he wanted to be wheeled into the reception area so he could talk to the patients. He was still euphoric after office hours, and we took him out for a short wheelchair ride before supper. After his evening meal, he watched a ballgame on TV and again slept soundly.

This routine continued smoothly for almost a week. Dad was weak, and he napped every afternoon, but he appreciated the privacy of not having his vital signs taken twenty-four hours a day. He also rested easier knowing we were close by. Although he must have been in constant pain, he requested very little medication.

To make things easier for him, we gave Dad a sleeping pill at bedtime, which he thought was for pain. The whole staff spoiled him during the day, and Nancy gave him back rubs at night. He seemed to be happy and getting stronger every day.

At suppertime on Tuesday, May 6, Dad was in particularly good spirits. He'd talked on the phone that day with my mother, and my sister called to say she was coming to see him the next day. Nancy had prepared his favorite dinner—roast beef and potatoes—and we'd spread a cloth on the table in the reception area. After he'd cleaned his plate, we wheeled him outside where we talked and watched the traffic.

Later, Paul brought a newborn puppy to show his granddaddy. We'd never seen Dad's smile so big. He told Paul, "I want you to take care of my car for me." The 1974 Chevrolet Impala was Dad's most prized possession. He'd paid cash for it the morning after his other car had burned.

It was Nancy's turn to spend that night at the office while I was on call at the hospital. She phoned to say Dad was restless and mumbling. She stayed up with him all night as he continued to mumble, but she couldn't understand a word. We began to fear he'd had a stroke.

When I got to the office the next morning, Nancy was exhausted, but Dad was sleeping peacefully. Earlier, he'd asked for a glass of water in a clear voice, which seemed a good sign. I sent Nancy home.

I checked on him between patients, but he continued to sleep. About 9:30, he rang his bell, and I went to him. In a clear voice, he said he wasn't hungry, but would like some juice. When I brought it to him, he looked contented and peaceful. "You know that Nancy and I love you very much," I said. "It shows," he replied, and he went back to sleep.

A little while later, when my nurse asked me to check on Dad, he wasn't breathing. It was over.

We were grateful that we could take care of him as long as we did. It isn't often that you can fulfill someone's last wish. My father died with dignity, with an alert mind, and surrounded by love. Can anyone ask for more?

ANDREW H. MALCOLM

The first memory I have of him—of anything, really—is his strength. It was in the late afternoon in a house under construction near ours. The unfinished wood floor had large, terrifying holes whose yawning darkness I knew led to nowhere good. His powerful hands, then age thirty-three, wrapped all the way around my tiny arms, then age four, and easily swung me up to his shoulders to command all I surveyed.

The relationship between a son and his father changes over time. It may grow and flourish in mutual maturity. It may sour in resented dependence or independence. With many children living in single-parent homes today, it may not even exist.

But to a little boy right after World War II, a father seemed a god with strange strengths and uncanny powers enabling him to do and know things that no mortal could do or know. Amazing things, like putting a bicycle chain back on, just like that. Or building a hamster cage. Or guiding a jigsaw so it formed the letter F; I learned the alphabet that way in those pre-television days, one letter or number every other evening plus a review of the collection. (The vowels we painted red because they were special somehow.)

He even seemed to know what I thought before I did. "You look like you could use a cheeseburger and chocolate shake," he would say on hot Sunday afternoons. When, at the age of five, I broke a neighbor's garage window with a wild curve ball and waited in fear for ten days to make the announcement, he seemed to know about it already and to have been waiting for something.

There were, of course, rules to learn. First came the handshake. None of those fishy little finger grips, but a good firm squeeze accompanied by an equally strong gaze into the other's eyes. "The first thing anyone knows about you is your handshake," he would say. And we'd practice it each night on his return from work, the serious toddler in the battered Cleveland Indians cap running up to the giant father to shake hands again and again until it was firm enough.

When my cat killed a bird, he defused the anger of a nine-year-old with a little chat about something called "instinked." The next year, when my dog got run over and the weight of sorrow was just too immense to stand, he was there, too, with his big arms and his own tears and some thoughts on the natural order of life and death, although what was natural about a speeding car that didn't stop always escaped me.

As time passed, there were other rules to learn. "Always do your best." "Do it now." "NEVER LIE!" And, most importantly, "You can do whatever you have to do." By my teens, he wasn't telling me what to do anymore, which was scary and heady at the same time. He provided perspective, not telling me what was around the great corner of life but letting me know there was a lot more than just today and the next, which I hadn't thought of.

When the most important girl in the world—I forget her name now—turned down a movie date, he just happened to walk by the kitchen phone. "This may be hard to believe right now," he said, "but someday you won't even remember her name."

One day, I realize now, there was a change. I wasn't trying to please him so much as I was trying to impress him. I never asked him to come to my football games. He had a high-pressure career, and it meant driving through most of Friday night. But for all the big games, when I looked over at the sideline, there was that familiar fedora. And, by God, did the opposing team captain ever get a firm handshake and a gaze he would remember.

Then, a school fact contradicted something he said. Impossible that he could be wrong, but there it was in the book. These accumulated over time, along with personal experiences, to buttress my own developing sense of values. And I could tell we had each taken our own, perfectly normal paths.

I began to see, too, his blind spots, his prejudices and his weaknesses. I never threw these up at him. He hadn't to me, and, anyway, he seemed to need protection. I stopped asking his advice; the experiences he drew from no longer seemed relevant to the decisions I had to make. On the phone, he would go on about politics at times, why he would vote the way he did or why some incumbent was a jerk. And I would roll my eyes to the ceiling and smile a little, though I hid it in my voice.

He volunteered advice for a while. But then, in more recent years, politics and issues gave way to talk of empty errands and, always, to ailments—his friends', my mother's and his own, which were serious and included heart disease. He had a bedside oxygen tank, and he would ostentatiously retire there during my visits, asking my help in easing his body onto the mattress. "You have very strong arms," he once noted.

From his bed, he showed me the many sores and scars

on his misshapen body and all the bottles for medicine. He talked of the pain and craved much sympathy. He got some. But the scene was not attractive. He told me, as the doctor had, that his condition would only deteriorate. "Sometimes," he confided, "I would just like to lie down and go to sleep and not wake up."

After much thought and practice ("You can do whatever you have to do."), one night last winter, I sat down by his bed and remembered for an instant those terrifying dark holes in another house thirty-five years before. I told my father how much I loved him. I described all the things people were doing for him. But, I said, he kept eating poorly, hiding in his room and violating other doctors' orders. No amount of love could make someone else care about life, I said; it was a two-way street. He wasn't doing his best. The decision was his.

He said he knew how hard my words had been to say and how proud he was of me. "I had the best teacher," I said. "You can do whatever you have to do." He smiled a little. And we shook hands, firmly, for the last time.

Several days later, at about 4 A.M., my mother heard Dad shuffling about their dark room. "I have some things I have to do," he said. He paid a bundle of bills. He composed for my mother a long list of legal and financial what-to-do's "in case of emergency." And he wrote me a note.

Then he walked back to his bed and laid himself down. He went to sleep, naturally. And he did not wake up.

ERIC LAX

I liked my father a lot. He was funny and warm and does not seem to have burdened me with much of the excess baggage parents sometimes heap on their children. His name was John. A few people, my mother included, called him Jack. When she was mad at him she called him JACKLAX!

On his seventy-first birthday he looked like this: five feet six inches with thinned black and gray hair. A tanned bald spot atop his head atop a tanned body with a generous, though not often excessive, girth; until he was about fifty he was very thin. Trifocals for his nearly black eyes. A weathered face, laugh lines. The middle two fingers on his left hand were mostly missing, the result of an accident when he was twelve at the coal mine of which my grandfather was foreman. An old joke of his was to hold up his left hand and say, "Three beers." Try to picture it.

He was born in Swallownest, England, a village of a few hundred in southern Yorkshire, the youngest of six children. My grandfather told my father that he would be an architect. My father told my grandfather that he would be no such thing; he was going to be an Anglican priest and the hell with everyone. When he was twenty-four he left England and went to the seminary in Saskatchewan. When my father was in the seminary he liked to play jokes. One involved fixing a device to the steering column of a Model A so that it could be guided by appropriate leg movements. He then loosened the wheel so that as he drove along a country road, he could pull it off and hand it to the passenger, saying, "Here, you drive."

After he left the seminary he and another priest whom he always referred to as Smithy shared a house. My father had a parish of 47,000 square miles and far fewer people, whom he tended like a circuit judge. It being the Depression, he received virtually no money, only food from various members of the congregation. He ate a dozen eggs a day for three years. He claimed that he used butter for axle grease because it was cheaper and was going to waste, and that the antifreeze in his car was often bootleg liquor that had been confiscated by the local Mountie. He was also very friendly during that time with a Chinaman who taught him how to belch after a meal, although he never said whether he taught the Chinaman anything. . . .

When I was told my father had cancer I made an unsurprising decision: I would spend more time with him. I had seen little of my parents after I was eighteen. We got on well but I spent a couple of years in the Peace Corps, and there were a couple more years when I didn't see them because after they retired they traveled by freighter and camper around Europe and Australia. When they settled back near San Diego, where they had been for over twenty years, I was in New York.

The thing, of course, was to spend time with my father without making too big a deal out of it. We all knew that I was going to California every five or six weeks because of his likely impending death; yet I hoped that we would behave as normally as possible and that we would be able to say whatever things we had to say. I tried before each visit to think of questions I had never asked him. . . .

One afternoon I was sitting in the sun, making a show of doing work. We were not going to know the test results until the next afternoon and we shared an unspoken agreement that we would let each day take care of itself and not sit around wringing our hands. My father came out and pulled up a chair beside me.

"Let's face it," he said with little delay, "I'm not all that long for this world. I'm not afraid to die and I don't think it's going to happen for a while. But this will probably kill me. And it's not much of a life having no energy and being in pain anyway. So. I want to ask you to look out for your mother. That doesn't mean take full responsibility for her or move out here or anything like that. Just look out for her, okay?" So this is what it's like, I thought. Your father comes out into the sunshine and asks that you look out for your mother after he dies. And as much: Look out for yourself.

"How about a beer," he said then.

When the phone rang the next afternoon my mother was outside, my father and I were reading in the living room. "You answer it," he said in his strained whisper, "my voice isn't strong enough."

There were no surprises. It was the doctor. The cancer had gone to his bones. My father would be given chemotherapy but the outlook was bleak. "We can do a lot to reduce the pain," the doctor told me, "but he has four, maybe five months at best. Bring him in tomorrow afternoon and I'll show him the scans and X-rays and explain what we do next."

For weeks afterward I was not certain which was worse, telling my father that he would soon die or letting someone else do it. But really, who better than I to tell him?

"It was the doctor," I told him. "The cancer is in your bones. The tumor is spreading." In my head I was yelling at myself to keep my voice steady and my eyes dry. I half succeeded. My voice was half-steady. My eyes were half-dry. "They are going to give you chemotherapy and he says that will reduce the pain in your back. You're supposed to go in tomorrow and the doctor will explain everything." I was screaming at myself now to stay in control; the last thing either of us needed was for me not to finish. "I love you very much," I said with some evenness. "I don't think I could have had a better father." He nodded and looked calm. "Thank you, Son," he said, and we looked at each other for several seconds. Then, "Come on, split a beer with me."

We had a couple more that afternoon, too. When my mother came in my father told her the basics. No one said much else. We all moved out into the sun. My mother took a picture that afternoon. It is of my father, in a chaise longue, with the Pacific at his left hand, a glass of beer raised in his right, and a broad grin on his face.

I left California two or three days later, expecting that in a month or so I would go back, but in two weeks, the phone rang. It was one o'clock on a Tuesday morning. My father was in the hospital. He had collapsed while seeing the doctor. It would be a matter of hours, days at most, before his heart gave out. I talked with the doctor, I talked with my mother, I talked with my father.

"Well, I think this is it," he said in that near-voice.

"Just don't do anything rash until I get there."

"It'll be nice to see you. Here's Mother."

So I caught the first plane to San Diego and was by my father's bed by lunchtime. He looked awful. An oxygen tube was in his nose, an intravenous tube in his arm. His color was gray, which matched the food on his plate. Beside the bed was a copy of *Alice in Wonderland.*

"Hi, Son," he said. "Here, have some of this food. I can't eat it all."

Who could? The sugar package had a picture of the Torrey Pines golf course on one side. On the other it said, "Enjoy yourself! You're dining in the playground of Southern California."

There is not much to talk about with someone who is concentrating on staying alive, but we had plenty to distract us. My father was not a stranger to this hospital. For more than twenty years he had been going there to see people and to give last rites and comfort families. So doctors and nurses who knew him popped in, and a lab technician who noticed his name on a vial came up, and various clergymen he knew came and went after leaving a prayer floating over the bed. As for me, I wandered in and out. My father didn't want me just sitting around on some sort of deathwatch and neither did I. So I went for walks, called friends in New York in the hope of easing my pain and fear, sat by him for a spell. After he toyed with his dinner my mother and I went to a nearby restaurant. She had spent the night sitting by his bed but she was calm and ready for whatever was to happen. One thing that was going to happen, my father told her, was that she was going home that night with me. Over dinner I told her that I wanted her to come to New York for a visit as soon as she was ready, and she said she would. This all went so smoothly. Like being underwater.

Before going home, though, my mother took a walk while my father and I talked.

"If you take the Bible and look closely, you'll see that Christianity comes down to only one thing," he said. "That is to love one another. That's what counts. Love one another." And then he repeated something he told me one night a couple of years after he had retired and we were leaning on the bar at the George and Dragon, a pub my mother's grandmother's family had owned, three miles from where my father grew up. "The Church is filled with people who should never be priests. They have their heads buried completely away from the world. They don't know how to deal with sex or drugs or any of the other real things that are part of life. They spout platitudes and hide behind dogma. When I retired and started hearing sermon after sermon, week after week, in church after church, by someone who was simply incompetent, I could only hope I wasn't that foolish or scared. As for the Church, it is more Big Business than it is Christianity."

Advice was something my father seldom gave, and this was notable for a clergyman. When I was five he did advise strongly that I take some medicine or else, and because I hated the medicine I took the or else (and later the medicine). But other than things like that there were really few pieces of advice he gave me. One occurred just before I went away to college. My father took me aside, as I had expected, and said, as I had not expected, "Now, Son, if a strange woman ever comes up to you on the street and offers to take your watch around the corner and have it engraved, don't do it."

It would be dramatic but untrue to say that my mother and I slept with an ear open for the phone; we slept like stones. When we got to the hospital my father was in decent spirits after an uncomfortable night. He needed a shave but with his tubes and general weakness couldn't handle it himself. So I took an electric razor and did it for him, remembering that on Saturday mornings when I was about seven my father and I would go into the bathroom, where he would run his shaving brush around the soap bowl and lather his face and I would take an old brush and do the same. Then we would shave—he with a new blade, I with an empty razor.

The following morning an attendant came into the room to check the oxygen flow to my father. "This is set too high," he announced, and turned it way down. I asked him to turn it back up and check his information; I had been there when the doctor said it should go so high. Another attendant came in, followed by a nurse. They argued about whether the flow should be up or down. My father complained that water was condensing in his nose from the oxygen, so one of the attendants took the nosepiece off to change it. The debate over pressure continued. My father began to look like a fish out of water. "Get the oxygen back to him immediately," I nearly screamed. The tube was replaced but the oxygen pressure was not elevated. One attendant stayed behind while the other went to check. He finally returned and put the flow up as high as it had been. I wanted to kill them all. . . .

. . . A few hours later I drove home to get the mail and run a couple of errands. I called the hospital before going back to see if I should bring anything. "Just yourself," my mother said. "Your father's having trouble."

I drove the seven miles to the hospital in fewer minutes, rehearsing all the way what I would say to the highway patrolman who might stop me for doing ninety on the freeway, but it turned out to be a speech I can save. The figures in my father's room were a deathbed tableau. Two nurses bent over him, one with a blood-pressure collar, another holding his arm. My mother held his hand. "Let me go," he was saying, clearly to the nurses, "let me go."

"Hi, Dad," I said.

He opened his eyes. "Oh, hello, Son." The nurses backed off as I went to the other side of the bed. My father rolled over to greet me. I caught him in my arms. Within a few minutes his body had rattled itself quiet.

Two days ago I returned from a weekend in San Francisco to learn that my father had died.

Sam Prelutsky had been born in Russia, in 1901 or 1902. He never knew for certain. It didn't seem to bother him.

As a young man in America, he settled in a part of Illinois where the most popular organization going was the Ku Klux Klan. After the Cossacks, though, I guess a bunch of farmers wearing sheets weren't such a big deal. Years later, he used to laugh about his former neighbors inviting him—*him* with his nose and his accent—on Klan outings. Maybe they had decided to overlook the obvious evidence in the belief that Jewish people didn't raise chickens or candle eggs.

Later, after he was married, he moved to Chicago. For a while he worked for a cigar company, rolling the stogies he couldn't stand to smoke. But for most of the time, he was a fruit and vegetable wholesaler. He'd drive his truck to the big central market at 3 A.M., pick up his load, and spend the next twelve hours delivering produce. In the dead of winter, he'd be out on that truck, *shlepping* sacks of potatoes. In the middle of summer, he'd be muscling crates of watermelons—just begging for the hernia he eventually got.

In '46, we moved to L.A. At that point he came to the conclusion that the people he'd been delivering to over the years had been living the life of Riley, home in bed, snoozing, while he was up *shlepping*. He decided to tackle the retail end. A few months at a bad location ate up most of his savings, and sent him back to the truck. But L.A., massive sprawl that it was even then, was murder compared to Chicago.

His next venture was a cigar stand in the Harris-Newmark Building, at Ninth and Los Angeles. Not counting the drive, it was still a twelve-hour day, spent mostly on his feet. But at least the lifting and carrying was limited to soft drink cases and trash barrels. On the other hand, you had to learn to live with the *goniffs* who swiped candy bars during the noon rush, and the merchant princes of the garment industry who'd run up good-sized cigar bills and let you stew until they were ready to pay up. And my father would stew because he couldn't afford to offend the pot-bellied, cigar-chewing, fanny-pinching, sweat shop aristocrats.

He was not an educated man. He couldn't correctly spell the names of those sodas and candy bars he sold six days a week. I don't know if he read two dozen books in his life. He loved America, Israel, pinochle, F.D.R., and the Democratic Party. He liked Willkie, Kuchel, and Warren, but he could never bring himself to vote for a Republican.

He wanted me to get good grades, a college degree and have a profession—something safe, and preferably lucrative, like medicine or the law. He couldn't understand someone's wanting to write. Still, when I sold a poem at the age of thirteen for fifty cents, he cashed the check for me—and later I found out he always carried that undeposited check around in his wallet.

Yesterday we went to the mortuary. We went through the ritual of selecting a casket. "They start at three hundred dollars," the salesman informed us, pointing at something that looked like an old Thom McAn shoebox, "and go up." We passed on the coffin that costs as much as a new Cadillac, and settled on an oak box that you could swap for a '67 Chevy.

Then we had to sit there, while some dame gathered data for the cosmetician. We tried to explain that it was to be a closed-casket ceremony, but she had not been programmed to receive such information. "Did he wear clear nail polish?" (No, he never wore nail polish. But had he worn nail polish, it would have been clear as opposed to purple or fire engine red.)

It was finally spelled out for her that they could save their rouge and polish and stupid questions. She turned pale at our impertinence. Her shock was reassuring; up to that point I had regarded her as a robot.

This afternoon, we buried my father. I didn't think I would, but I shed tears. I cried because he had worked too hard for too long for too little. For many years I had resented him because he had never told me he loved me; now I wept because I'd never told him.

The rabbi's speech was short and simple. What is there, after all, to say at the funeral of such a man? Had the responsibility been mine, I would have said, *Sam Prelutsky, who was born in a small village seven thousand miles from here, sixty-seven or sixty-eight years ago, was a remarkable person. He was not a great man, but he was the very best man Sam Prelutsky could be. Now, let there be no more tears today—for we are laying to rest a man who's earned one.*

7

Remembering

RICH COWLES / STEVE LaRUE

DAVID S. POWELL / RAYMOND CARVER

CHRISTOPHER HALLOWELL / PAUL WILKES

CLARK BLAISE / BROCK BROWER

PAUL ZWEIG / DAVID IGNATOW

RICH COWLES

People thought my dad was a claims attorney for an insurance company. But they didn't grow up in his house. He was a philosopher.

Dressed in mismatched apparel from another era, he would slouch in his living room chair and muse about life as if from an observation post. While deep in thought, the philosopher would tap out his special rhythm with his scuffed brown shoes. It was nothing fancy—a catchy little beat with a slight syncopation—but it was constant and natural, and it was his own personal rhythm. My dad's musing and tapping provided a reassuring accompaniment to my childhood. No matter how frightening or unfair life became, he could put it in perspective with the long view from his observation post. Everything would be O.K.

As I grew older, I liked to join my dad at his post. Together we philosophized about life's unanswered questions and tried to find meaning in the world's random injustice. There was an unpolished grace about the way he'd slouch in his chair and observe today's burden as but an incidental blight in life's broad landscape. Sadness is a part of life, he would conclude, and remind me of the hidden power of our "inner strength." To acknowledge that life can get mean, to look past it and keep on tapping, is to rise above the pain.

I find myself drumming my dad's rhythm these days, as if it could help me rise above the pain and return order to my life . . . as if it could bring him back. On an ordinary night a few weeks ago, without fanfare or ceremony, a massive cardiac arrest put an end to my dad's tapping.

I wake in the night and know instantly the accompaniment is missing. Gone is the steady beat that could make everything O.K. Gone is the assuredness that there is a person who believes in me no matter what and with whom I share a common view of the universe from the observation post.

I've been on my own for many years now, but I still turned to my dad at sign posts. When my mother died, he helped me accept our loss, not through pat answers but through the long view of the philosopher. Now there is no one to call on. Now there's no one between me and death. When I saw my dad lying gray and still and permanent, when there was no parental hand to soothe the sting, I realized the part of me that was son is dead now too. Now I'm strictly father.

That's not all bad. I've received comfort from the noisy tribe that calls me "Dad." It seems that ninety-nine percent of the time you talk to the people with whom you live about things that don't matter. In fact, most of the time that our entire family's together, we shovel in food while grunting primitively. But I discovered that, in matters of life and death, behind the shoveling and grunting are pure and genuine hearts. My fifteen- and fourteen-year-old boys' efforts to keep me company when I look sad are a heartwarming giant step beyond normal teen-age behavior. Even my six-year-old understands that I've lost something important. She's taken on a nurturing role, and I felt my knees go weak the night I tucked her into bed and she whispered, "I feel sorry for you, Dad."

I've always felt an easy comfort in my role as link between my father and my children. Now the break in the genealogical chain troubles me. It is the burden that seems more than an incidental blight in the big picture; it is the source of the pain that clouds the long view. Now my father becomes a mere historical figure to my children— particularly to the youngest, not even two years old. I understand the emptiness of that kind of relationship. I know my grandfather only as legend, built from my dad's stories, which he often ended plaintively with "I wish you could have known him." My youngest will not remember the shy smiles she and her grandpa exchanged from across the room, the way he'd give her time to warm up to him and his eventual squeeze.

My daughter will know him only from my stories. I will tell her that her grandpa taught me that a person could be both male and gentle. He taught me, many years ago, as he sat on my bed and patiently helped me understand there was nothing to fear in the dark. He taught me when he, the pull-yourself-up-by-your-bootstraps-Republican of the family, cried as they played taps for John Kennedy. He taught me in the way he sensed I was unprepared when my mother's cancer went on the rampage. He took me aside and told me ever so gently, "We must steel ourselves for the worst."

I will tell how my dad carefully chiseled out a niche as the family eccentric, exemplified in the rituals he went through to ward off a cold, which, if unsuccessful, leveled him for days. A magic potion in this ritual was citrus, which he ingested while reminding us of the miserable cold he'd caught while shipside in the navy. He'd lived on nothing but oranges for four days and, presto, the scourge magically disappeared, thereby proving the effectiveness of the wonder fruit. I never had the heart to suggest that many self-respecting colds don't expect to live longer than four days.

My dad wasn't strong when it came to colds and other nettlesome bothers of life. In later years, he seemed unnecessarily irritated by them. Yet when he'd take to his observation post to deal with life's mortal wounds, he was an iron man. In the last few months he talked frequently about the old days and friends who were no longer living. I see now he was preparing himself and those he loved for when he would "cash in his chips." Even his wry euphemism was a form of acceptance.

I know now that a week before he died, my dad confided in his new wife that his time was near. Yet the letter he wrote to my brother hours before he died shows this knowledge hadn't changed him. He was still looking ahead. Writing about the upcoming birthday party for two of his grandchildren, the final words he wrote were, "We plan to go."

I can hear him saying that. I hear his voice stronger and more insistent these days. It is the voice of the philosopher from the observation post, telling me that life may pause, but it never stops. The voice is telling me, gently but earnestly, that life's good days should be spent looking ahead. It is telling me to tap out my own accompaniment and finish life's song without him.

STEVE LaRUE

Dad waged a constant and, by his accounts, an heroically futile war against shoddy workmanship and pot metal. He dated the beginning of the decline of American civilization from the date the factories stopped galvanizing nails by passing current through them, permanently bonding the protective zinc, and fell instead to merely dipping the nails in molten zinc, which staves off corrosion for only several years.

Dad could stare in pain at sheet metal gutters he'd hammered onto the roof a decade ago and read the steady decline of America in the rusty streams bleeding from each decomposing nailhead.

My father built to last. He didn't build for style, God knows not for convenience or beauty, and not for comfort. He was an engineer and he built to last.

Since he bought our first home in the late 1940s, in Massachusetts, the rest of us always joked that whatever Dad built around the house could withstand a direct hit by an atomic bomb.

He seemed to spend much of his time around the house in those early years trying to divine the hidden location of studs—those two-by-four wall supports hidden under the plaster every sixteen inches. He would tap the wall and listen, then sink a test nail. He'd grunt with satisfaction when he found one, then drill a hole and lovingly crank lag bolts through the plaster and deep into the sturdy wood beneath, anchoring shelves and picture frames irrevocably and, it seemed, forever.

Forever came one Saturday in May, 1990. Dad died in his sleep early that morning after a routine Friday doing some of the things he liked best. He'd dismantled an innocent piece of machinery and put the parts into an unlabeled coffee can, one of dozens of unlabeled, parts-filled cans we would find around the house in the next weeks. He'd talked to one of his three children on the phone, and with the Canadian branch of the family in another call. In both, he'd found some occasion to share a laugh.

He'd demolished a plate of fresh fish for dinner, and he'd watched a baseball game on TV with his wife. Their team, the Oakland A's, had won. There is seldom a good time to die, but there are worse ways.

Stunned, my two sisters and I gathered at our family's San Francisco Peninsula home of thirty-five years to pick up and put away our father's tools and sort through the relics of his life.

There were Dad's college football spikes, bent and brittle but still caked with the now crystallized mud of a long-ago gridiron in upstate New York, where he played his last game in 1941.

There was a basketball play book, filled with scores and newspaper clips from a YMCA team, where he played in his teens during the Depression, when he wasn't driving a bakery truck in Massachusetts.

Missing were his old baseball spikes, which I first saw slung over his shoulder as he towered over me at the kitchen door in Massachusetts, with his four-fingered pitcher's mitt under his arm and a smile on his face. He was a right-handed junkballer who could usually get the curve over the plate but not the fastball. For most pitchers, it's just the opposite, but that seems to fit.

Most of the vital records of his life were in an ammunition box from World War II. Under a stack of twenty-year-old amateur radio magazines and decades of dust, I found a copy of his 1950s patent for a kind of magnetron, the tube at the heart of radar sets. Dad got the patent; Raytheon Corp. got the millions it was worth.

In the room he called his radio shack, there were notes thanking him for using his high-powered ham radio and the 150-foot antenna that so infuriated the neighbors to link Bay Area families with distant relatives after the October 1989 earthquake, and with servicemen in Vietnam. He paid the phone tolls himself.

Mother was moving, so the stereo cabinet Dad built two decades ago had to be flattened to be taken to the dump. It must have weighed two hundred pounds, minus the components—thick marine plywood, screwed and glued, with an ugly Formica veneer.

My new brother-in-law swung a heavy sledge at it, and the hammer bounced into the air like a tennis ball without making a dent. I smiled quietly. It took five or six mighty blows from a strong man before the wood began to crack.

"Sorry, Dad," I said to myself, no longer smiling.

Dad didn't do finish work. He poured the foundation, framed in the walls, lashed up the rough plumbing, and that was about it. He and I built an addition onto the house in 1965. There's still no shower. I installed the bathroom door and the carport light a few weeks after he died.

But he was a master with concrete, and the various slabs he poured around the place might last as long as the Pyramid of Cheops. One thing, they won't go as easily as his stereo cabinet. To build new homes, the developer who buys my parents' lot will have to demolish and haul off the concrete foundation of the backyard shop and radio shack Dad and I built. He'll assume the slab is about three inches thick, and plan to haul it off in a day or two.

Good luck. I know different because I was chief slave on the project in 1957. The floor is twice that thick, with steel reinforcing rods every fourteen inches, and steel mesh. The edge of the foundation is several feet thick with more reinforcing bars and mesh.

Nothing but jackhammers and cutting torches are going to budge it. There's going to be a lot of swearing, and it could take them weeks to remove it. That would tickle Dad. It already has—we laughed about it at least once a year after we finished the project.

After he died, I began to see much more clearly that my father did not work only in electronics and concrete. My sisters, my mother and I had grown apart, and some of us thought we basically didn't get along and wouldn't spend time together but for the family.

After Dad died, we saw that our lives are lag-bolted and soldered together as permanently as any of his other home projects, even if we did have to do our own finish work for ourselves. Steel reinforced, we've survived a direct hit, and we feel we will endure. That would tickle him, too.

This thought came to me one night, back home in San Diego, as I was trying to hang Dad's framed Merchant Marine license in my home. I found myself tapping the wall board. I was looking for the studs.

DAVID S. POWELL

Every Christmas for nearly thirty years, my father wrote one of those holiday form letters and tucked it inside our family's Christmas card. And every year those letters seemed the same to me: a predictable distillation of our family's routine activities—activities that varied so little from year to year that no updates ever really seemed necessary. I read each Christmas letter in turn but never considered saving them. After all, I had *lived* all this stuff. Why relive what had seemed so dull the first time around?

Strangely enough, it's not dull anymore.

My father died a year ago last May, and this past Christmas my sister, who has always been more foresighted than I, gave me copies of the annual letters she had saved—the ones Dad wrote from 1964 to 1988. What was once boring to me is fascinating now. Both fascinating and precious.

It's not because the news in these letters has improved with age. Quite the contrary. The activities are still routine —health reports, job news, vacation anecdotes—typical happenings common to typical American families. Even the special occasions, the weddings, births, divorces, and deaths, are reduced to little more than a sentence or two. I guess that there's just no other way to sum up the experiences of six people on one or two pages.

But it's not the words that matter now; it's what I see between the lines. These holiday missives tell far more about their author than they do about their subjects. Reading them now, fifteen or twenty years removed in time, I can see and hear my father on every page, in ways I never could have noticed before when I was younger, even if he had been able to show me.

I was just a kid when Dad composed most of these letters —a kid who was kept blissfully ignorant of adult problems and parental responsibilities. Oh, I knew my father had health problems, and the annual letters chronicled them faithfully, if lightheartedly. Over the years there were glib references to each of three coronary-bypass operations; there were brief and dutiful notations on the effects of diabetes, emphysema, phlebitis, arteriosclerosis. But they were just words on a page, big words that had very little impact on me at the time. These health problems hadn't seemed to affect Dad much. He had suffered from them since my earliest recollections, yet he always seemed to be the same funny, sensible, approachable guy I had always known.

Even in 1975, the year in which the terrible pressures of his middle-management job pushed him to the edge of a nervous breakdown and, finally, into retirement, he seemed to gloss over these things in his Christmas letter. He didn't *want* to retire; I knew that. But his letter made a joke out of retirement, and I had no trouble laughing along. At the time, I was a twenty-year-old, newly married college kid, far too full of my own concerns (and of myself, I suppose) to have time for Dad's problems with health and work, particularly when he did such a good job of concealing them from us.

Today I'm a thirty-five-year-old man with a fifteen-year marriage and two children of my own. Now *I'm* struggling with middle-management pressures. Now *I* chart my cholesterol levels and worry about retirement funds and college expenses. Reading these letters with more experienced eyes, I can finally see that Dad's jokes masked real pain, real fear, real regret. I can see that his early retirement was a crushing blow to his ego. To a man who had supported his family for nearly thirty years, disability retirement must have felt a lot like failure, failure caused by weakness. Thanks to his letters, I know Dad better now than I ever did when he was alive.

RAYMOND CARVER

PHOTOGRAPH OF MY FATHER IN HIS TWENTY-SECOND YEAR

October. Here in this dank, unfamiliar kitchen
I study my father's embarrassed young man's face.
Sheepish grin, he holds in one hand a string
of spiny yellow perch, in the other
a bottle of Carlsbad beer.

In jeans and denim shirt, he leans
against the front fender of a 1934 Ford.
He would like to pose bluff and hearty for his posterity,
wear his old hat cocked over his ear.
All his life my father wanted to be bold.

But the eyes give him away, and the hands
that limply offer the string of dead perch
and the bottle of beer. Father, I love you,
yet how can I say thank you, I who can't hold my liquor
    either,
and don't even know the places to fish?

CHRISTOPHER HALLOWELL

. . . I wander into the living room and turn to the fire-place mantel, an unconscious movement that I catch my-self doing each time I come to the house after a long absence. I turn toward my father, the most dominant force in my life when I was a boy and still influential though dead for eight years. He stares at me from two fading photo-graphs. I stare back, hoping to discover some chink in his expression that I have not noticed before, a suggestion in the deep-set eyes of why he held such power and so blithely abused it. I see nothing new. The way he is in the photo-graphs is how I remember him so often. In one, he is racing the family sailboat, beating to windward, swells and whitecaps surrounding the little hull. His head is slightly inclined, and he is peering ahead with the intensity of a pointer staring down a bird. I know the pose. He is judging whether he can make the racing buoy on this tack or whether he will have to waste precious seconds by coming around and going off on the other. He is total concentra-tion and murmured monologue. "The tide is helping us, but we're getting into a chop. Now dammit, look at that boat over there. She's going like hell. Well, I don't know. If we stay here, we'll have to pinch her and lose too much. If we tack, we might just get an extra breeze. Hell, we'll tack. Ready about. Hardalee." Whether he tacks or not, he is constantly sailing right through the house's living room.

I could be in the boat with him, and was many times, huddled against the mast, soaked and shivering, thinking that this kind of racing must be the slowest sport known to man. But for him the weekend races were the meat of his upbringing. Winning the race brought a delusion of total acceptance.

In the other photograph, he is standing in the cockpit of a cruising boat. My mother took the picture; they were sailing with some friends of my father and had just come into a harbor for the night. He is wearing a grin that most people find charming. I know differently. He has just finished saying something sarcastic to my mother—perhaps about her persistent inability to operate a camera properly —and now he is waiting for her reaction of mock outrage. Behind the grin, he is angry. My mother hated sailing and feared boats, a fear that she could never overcome and that my father never understood.

Photographs of handsome old schooners that sailed out of my father's past decorate the walls of every room. Open a closet door and there hangs a suit of sails from one boat or another. The basement is full of salvaged gear—blocks and lines and stays and shackles—scrounged from minor wrecks delivered to the rocks in front of the house.

Dead these eight years, and the house is still in his name as is the post office box and the telephone listing. I wonder why I keep the photographs of him on the mantel. For several years after his death, I turned them down whenever I came to the house and felt guilty for doing so. But his face would not go away. Now I just leave them there and happily realize that the pain he caused is gradually diminishing each year. . . .

. . . Our last confrontation was on Weenaumet Point early one winter after a snowfall. By that time, my father had suffered three heart attacks and two strokes. He had recovered from each one, though they had diminished his outward fire. I was shoveling snow, and the blade caught on the edge of a wooden step and splintered it. Just as writing was my net, the house was my father's. He heard the sound and saw that I had damaged the one thing in his life that he felt proud of. Once again, he yelled at me. He ridiculously accused me of intentionally destroying his house. I realized then the extent of the fear with which he regarded me, the possibility that his son might sweep him off his feet by chipping away at his only crutch. For years, my mother had told me how jealous he had grown of me. Here was the proof.

"I am not destroying your house," I screamed at him. "You're scared that I will destroy you."

He looked baffled; my father was a man of little psychological insight. "I saw what you did to those steps," he snapped. But his eyes flitted from mine as he said it.

I felt sad then. "You're not angry at me about the steps; just a splinter of wood came off. You're mad at me because I have gone far beyond your image of me. You're mad because I am young and I am going away. You're mad because you have lived in fear all your life and never been able to admit it to anyone."

His face turned white. He clutched the back of a chair, and I thought that he was going to have another heart attack. He stared at me with tearful eyes. "Yes," he murmured. "And now I am scared of dying." That was the most honest and revealing thing he ever said to me.

Two weeks later, a large package was delivered to my apartment in New York. I was preparing to set off for Louisiana to begin research on my first book, the one about the Mississippi River delta. The package contained a much-needed electric typewriter. There was no message. I knew it was a terribly silent effort by my father to help me in my writing. It was also an acknowledgment of my escape.

Three weeks later, he was dead. . . .

Weenaumet is a good place to test a reconciliation. It is impossible to escape my father here. There is the knotty pine covering the walls. There is the fireplace; he laid its bricks. He built the beds that we sleep upon and the railing bench that overhangs the deck. When I see a Herreschoff beating to windward in the bay, the figure at the helm could easily be he. And there is the flagpole. The community erected it in my father's memory near what some residents here call the yacht club but others more honestly refer to as the boathouse, a one-room shack toward the back of the beach. With all the understatement that typifies Weenaumet, the brass plaque on the pole reads: BILL HALLOWELL, 1906–1978. The flags fluttering aloft are as much a local fixture as my father was. . . .

A month in the house has turned its shipshape orderliness to chaos. Cleaning is an all-day ordeal. In the process we come upon articles of the kids' clothing that have been missing for days. I also discover something that startles me.

The basement is full of paraphernalia accumulated by my father. He never threw anything away. After he died, we came upon bank statements going back fifty years. Hooks and nails are draped with lengths of rope and electrical wiring that he collected. The space between the ceiling joists and house beams holds caches of lead fishing weights, golf balls, and boxes of shackles. Timbers of various dimensions and heights lean against the walls. Many have fallen or are askew, making the place look like the periphery of a lumberyard. I decide to straighten them up, not throw them out, for, like my father, I have found that such odds and ends are always useful, though they may rest untouched for years.

Matthew hears me crashing around and comes to investigate with a cheerful "I thought there was a monster in the basement making all that noise. Dad, are you a monster?" Then he begins to help me. In one corner, a pile of six-by-twelves leans crookedly against the wall. Sawed-off beam ends left over from the construction of the house, they have been there since it was finished sixteen years ago. They could stay there in disarray, but I am offended by their messy appearance, so I tell Matthew that our last job is to arrange the timbers so that they stand upright against the wall. Matthew runs to the task and begins heaving one of the beams upright. He can scarcely lift it but soon angles it upright away from its resting place. Then he calls to me. "Look, Dad, there's writing on the wall. What does it say?"

What is written on the concrete in barely distinguishable pencil is HOUSE FINISHED and underneath, AUGUST 1969. The writing is in my father's hand.

What made him commemorate the completion of the house by scrawling these words and numbers on the wall, I will never know. At least, I suppose that is what they signify. He certainly chose a humble means and untrafficked place. Then it struck me. He probably never wanted anyone to see the writing; he wrote it for himself, a private reminder that here was something at last that he had accomplished. In moments of unhappiness as the years went by, he may have come down here, pried away the beams, and gazed upon this crude inscription.

PAUL WILKES

My father was a tobacco-chewing carpenter, a man with a sixth-grade education, not the best sense of syntax or grammar, and I spent much of my life being ashamed of him. After all, he had false teeth, rough hands so ingrained with dirt that they never approached looking clean, and he never read anything more serious than the daily newspaper. I knew there was something more to life than the East Side of Cleveland, Ohio, and what later was called "blue collar" work, but I was equally certain that this man was not fit to be my guide into the larger world, of which I so badly wanted to be a part. Before I understood what the term "role model" meant, he was out of the running.

I didn't want my friends to meet him and hear subjects that never consulted their predicates. I'd always manage to be waiting in the driveway to be picked up. When I went to college and my fellow freshmen told me their fathers were "in" something like real estate or accounting or sales, my father suddenly was "in construction."

He wasn't a notable father in even the most rudimentary sense. I played three sports in grade school, but he never saw a game, never gave me a ride or told me he was proud it was my basket that beat St. Margaret's or my tackle that held Holy Rosary at the goal line. There was never to be that wonderful after-game scene with father walking toward the station wagon, arm draped over the huge shoulder pads that for an afternoon made his boy almost a man, confiding, "It's not who wins or loses, son, but how you. . . ."

He didn't teach me to catch a ball or encourage me to play sports, nor did he urge me on to college, or in any way urge me to better myself. He never lectured me, never *told* me anything. We never had a direct conversation, much less a heart-to-heart talk, so that I could learn what it was I needed to take along on a life's journey.

After all, he was just a working man who'd come through the Depression, sired and raised seven children, suffered the indignities of standing on food lines and having a house he'd built with those dirt-grimed hands taken away because he couldn't pay the few dollars of taxes. He stopped for a shot and a beer every night after work. Obviously, he had no wisdom or insights to impart from such an undistinguished life. . . .

. . . This year I asked myself: What did I learn from him that I want to pass on to my two sons? I came up with a modest list—of attitudes, really: about work and detachment, generosity and rage, and about square corners, that most central issue in every man's life.

WORK: He always got to the job before the other men who worked for the small construction company that employed him for twenty years. And he often was the last to leave, mumbling something under his breath about "Some bastard'll knock that over fer sure" as he shored up a side wall or nailed the last window casing in place. Did he do it for overtime pay or to impress the boss? Hardly.

"A man pay you fer eight hours work, you do nine," he'd say, not with any special pride, but simply because it was what an honest workingman did. It was an honor to be employed, a gift, and in his own way he acknowledged that every day.

. . .

DETACHMENT: He never criticized me when I almost failed out of college, and he never really congratulated me when my stories began to appear in a good number of national magazines. As emphysema, fed by coal dust in Pennsylvania and sawdust in Cleveland, gradually suffocated him, forcing him to spend his days at our worn breakfast-nook table, he'd take deep, wheezing breaths and pat a pile of dog-eared publications at his side. "I dunno; I guess Butch (he never once called me Paul) got some stories in 'em." It was as close as he would ever come to encouraging someone to read something I'd written, as he had obviously done many times.

GENEROSITY: With a mother-in-law (whom he detested), a wife and seven kids to support, he earned barely enough to cover our needs, but my father always felt that there was more than enough to go around. You had only to appear at our house anywhere close to mealtime, and he would insist you be fed. Roast beef or corn-meal mush: If we had it, you had it. If my father passed up seconds, saying he wasn't that hungry, it was one of the few times he might lie. And, if you came after 5 o'clock weekdays and any time on Saturday or Sunday, you'd be confronted with a frighteningly large shot glass of Corby's whiskey and a bottle of Erin Brew. The man was poor but he never thought of himself as poor.

A JUST RAGE: He was usually a mild-mannered man who worked quietly and never complained, even when his boss gave him the dirtiest, most odious part of one of their "fire jobs," reconstructing a burned-out store or residence. But when he got home too late and too woozy on Friday night and my mother counted out a slightly depleted pay envelope, he could be relied upon to put her in her place. "I beat my brains out all day and if I can't stop fer a little. . . ." He would take abuse on the job, sometimes the scorn of his family, but when a certain point was reached, my father would rise up in righteous indignation and reclaim his dignity.

SQUARE CORNERS: To watch him at work was to see a master carpenter. He seldom missed a nail, never gouged wood, even if it was interior framing that would soon be covered with wallboard. Corners were somehow mystically important to him, even those no one would see. I can recall him taking great pains to bevel perfectly the edges of two pieces of baseboard that would be all but hidden from view behind a huge and rather ugly radiator cover. The workday was over, and I was impatient for him to get finished, but he wouldn't do a slipshod job. "They ain't gonna know the difference, Butch, but this guy knows," he said, thumb pointed toward his chest. . . .

I am my father's son, and I know, whether it ever was a conscious or intentional decision, that I've tried to live by those truths he never told me. But, foolish man that I am, I didn't learn well enough. I find myself talking about the dignity of work and square corners to my older son, and I'm sure I'll blab on to the younger one, too, as soon as he'll listen. My words overstate my actions. My father did it beautifully, in reverse.

CLARK BLAISE

I was thirty-eight years old when my father died. I am now forty-five, but I don't feel I had thirty-eight years of fathering. In fact, I've heard more from my father these last seven years than I ever did when he was around.

He's on my mind because of the smell of cigarettes. He was a lifetime three-pack-a-day smoker, and his smoker's musk lingered over everything he touched. I was living in a furnished apartment in Atlanta, as Emory University's visiting writer, and the person who preceded me in that apartment had left his traces in the air, on the walls and in cigarette burns on the rim of the plastic bathtub. The edges of the dining table and kitchen counters were nicked with little brown parabolas where a butt had smoldered to its filter. Careless, hard-smoking people will be gone in a decade—it's hard to see them now as Bogarts and Hellmans after the Surgeon General has put them on notice. But they embody to me the low-rent heroism of people who know, better than most of us, their weakness, their foolishness and the price they're going to pay. I look on smokers as I look on my father now: foolish mortals, with stories to tell.

Seven years ago, my father was in a New Hampshire hospital, where I visited him every weekend from Montreal. He'd left Canada years before, tried Florida and Pittsburgh and several marriages, only to end his days in the French enclave of Manchester. His veins had collapsed, his feet were icy, he would never walk again. I had him where I wanted him. Now we could talk. Now he could hold my books, perhaps even read them, and he would tell me, finally, about his life, the epic novel that he'd lived.

His was the voice that had spoken to me whenever I wrote. I wanted him to know that. Through him and his stubborn fatalism, I made sense of my own heritage. The best book that I would ever be able to write would be *his* story, and I wanted him to start telling it. About Frenchness and hunger and death. About being the youngest of eighteen, seeing six siblings die in a single week, about the medieval Roman Catholicism of old Quebec. About his rum-running days during Prohibition, his prizefighting, his marriages. Such a simple thing to wonder about: do I have brothers and sisters? What made Leo Blais run, what made him into Lee Blaise, respectable Pittsburgh furniture dealer for a few years at least?

He'd had marriages before my mother; the father I remember was always in his fifties, always gray and turning white, thin on top, as I am now. When I was young, I was my mother's son, and until now I can say I was never his—intellectually, morally, physically. So why, in middle age, should I feel only his encoding? The face I sense looking out on the world is his. At forty-five, I'm in better shape than I've ever been, nearly in his ex-boxer's condition, without the side effects. I wouldn't shame him; we're a credible father and son now.

Like him, I left Canada, accepting risk for the hope of security. Risks both of us found, security never. He moved the family around the corners of America thirty-five times in twenty years—he was caged, there's no other metaphor—and it's with a certain terror that I realize I've registered my car in four different states in the last three years. Perhaps late blooming is encoded in both of us, along with the

DNA of wanderlust. Perhaps father and son had to try on several selves before settling on one they could live with.

I remember a day, long ago, on a central Florida street. We'd just come out of the bank, and I must have asked him for Coca-Cola money. He dug deep into the pocket of his high-waisted pants and came out with a handful of change. Forty cents or so. "That's it, son, that's all we've got." And it thrilled me; it was a sign. That meant we would make it, because that's how it turned out in the movies. You've got to be down before you can rise. All he had to do was hold on to his little house and the little job he had, and in ten years he would have become a millionaire, like all his friends. Six months later, he lost it all.

When he was nearly fifty, he began the lone successful operation of his life, a furniture store in Pittsburgh. We worked through a Pittsburgh summer converting a landmark restaurant into a furniture store, sealing up the old meat locker, boarding up the old fireplace. We presented the bank with a *fait accompli,* and they gave him a loan to stock the store. And the amazing thing, for a family that had known only insecurity and failure, was that for seven years it succeeded. It got me through college, before a new woman entered his life and, once again, he lost everything.

Besides the cigarettes, I remember now the lingering smell of stale meat and the acrid, encaked soot from the fireplace. That it should come down to this—a father, odors only! He died with his stories intact, and if I am to bring him back, I must reconstruct him from smoke and memories. As I enter my perilous years, I find that he is inside me, we are becoming one. His traces surround me, though his world is gone, or going fast. Middle age is the final orphanage.

BROCK BROWER

Seven years after my father's death, I have begun wearing his ring. Not always. I wear it, talismanically, to weddings, funerals and other solemnities, on long drives toward meaningful destinations. I slip it on, I will sheepishly admit, for its powers.

That is how it impressed me as a child. My father wore it most of the time, and was, of course, invincible. The band is stippled white gold with an inlay of red-gold bay leaves. The leaves curve up along both sides, like a tiny wreath entwined around the ring finger. The jewel is a semiprecious stone called a tiger's eye. The tiger's eye has the smoldering depth of a fierce stare, but it has been carved into a cameo. In blunt relief, an ancient warrior, helmeted, his visor up, juts a stern-jawed profile just below the knuckle. He does not look the least like my father, but surely comes from that same army of stalwart men.

Yet I remember my father often kept him turned around backward on his ring finger. That always puzzled me. Why hide this fierce-eyed warrior? Until, one day, with the ring on, I happened to reach into my pocket for some loose change and caught that jutting chin on the pocket's edge. It almost tore my pants. I find it happens every time. So I too have taken to twisting the ring around on my finger before reaching into my pocket, and it's easy enough to forget to twist it back again.

A small crotchet, but here I am, adopting his aura, his habits, his forgetfulness. It is as if the ring is casting a spell over its wearer, compelling him to behave as my father once did. I am at that advancing age, well into my fifties, when his few surviving friends say how much I am beginning to look like him (they used to say how much I took after my mother). I can catch a fleeting resemblance of him in the mirror. He is there in my surprised visage, scowling back at me, asking what have you got stuffed in your pockets now?

As a kid, I kept them bulging. They held all my secrets, if only acorns, old buckeyes, whole toothpicks, globs of clay. Later, there were better secrets, like stolen quarters, milling a guilty hole in the pocket seam, or captured material from local Dinky toy wars, or lurid sets of bubble-gum cards snugged into color-coded rubber bands. Once I even pocketed a three-dimensional puzzle of the Trylon and Perisphere from the 1939 World's Fair. I felt I had the whole world in my pocket, but I never told him.

Around that time, my father began giving me rides on his motorcycle, which he'd bought in his early forties, to my mother's horror. We sped through New Jersey's low Watchung Hills at breakneck clip. As I clutched the handlebars, I could see the ring over his tight grip around the throttle handle, grinding for real speed. We flashed past the traffic jams—a dynamic duo shielded by the ring's mysterious powers.

Later, we took up Broadway theater, the way other fathers and sons take up night baseball. Over the years, I'd say we saw the better performances under the lights— though the first star I recall loudly applauding was the invisible Harvey. I can still think of Harvey as a presence evoked by my father's ring. Through my college years, we took in *The Lady's Not for Burning*, Willy Loman, Annie Oakley and those strange English types who crashed T. S.

Eliot's *Cocktail Party.* I can see that ring's cameo set on the grip of the armrest between our adjoining theater seats, like a silhouette in tiny cartouche. Patron of the arts as well as warrior.

By then, my father was getting to be my current age. Entering his fifties, taking on those older lineaments that would fix him forever, in memory, as my father. He had very big hands, the right size for the ring. Settling into a chair, he would cross his long legs, then clasp both those hands over one raised knee and rock back against that hard-braced knee as he launched into some animated inquiry. I find myself doing the same, even at the dinner table. Then he would attempt some witticism, or pun, or joke on the point in question. I find I try even harder. Often enough, his point would be directed at me with a knowing look, and the eerie part is that I catch myself, lately, trying for that same knowing look.

In fact, I catch myself, in the midst of these half-conscious acts, going through an uncanny transformation. I sense myself coming under his intense scrutiny, but I am the one doing all his scrutinizing. It is not an out-of-body experience. It is deeply disorienting but undeniably enlightening to become one's own father. Through his eyes, with his wisdom and long patience and wry sympathy, I suddenly see myself for what I have become in his eyes.

And it is hard to keep anything from him. He still wants to know what I've got hidden away in my pockets, and I confess that the habit of sequestering my life lingers on. I still try to pocket secret worries, from unpaid bills I don't want to face, to the comb I use too often, along with how many other scraps of male vanity and head-of-household debts that bulge as large as ever.

That is why I am so careful about putting on my father's ring. I am convinced of its transforming powers, and know what sobering self-judgments those powers can bring down. I can sometimes feel my own forehead frowning his frown of disapproval at some unwarranted idleness or irresponsible venture, or new license I have taken up. And I know too well why he is so disapproving. I remember how he would rock back in his chair, keeping one hand locked with the other on his knee, at just my eye level, letting that warrior's glance fall full upon me. I know that hard look, straight from the knuckle.

Only that warrior is now on my ring finger. I am the one to direct his tiger's-eye stare. I looked down on his dark-jawed profile glinting at me, and sometimes I let him rest on my own knee. Or give him one good twist and snug him right into my pocket. But every time I go clumsily digging after my change, and forgetfully snag the set of that jaw again, I have to wonder: *Who is really reaching whose hand into whose pocket?*

PAUL ZWEIG

FATHER

I

I want to be near this mild unforgiving man,
Who comes from my hands and voice,
And is the nervous laughter
I hear before my throat expels it.

For years he slept days, worked nights,
Rode a bicycle when only boys did.
I remember his walks on the beach,
His face, so stubborn, so quiet, it frightened me,
Yet may only have been shy.

I imagine him hugging some gift
Along the Brooklyn streets when he was a boy,
Working at his father's laundry.
He preserved it in his mind,
A timeless falling world where he still lives.
And the gift was for me:
An amazed distance only acrobats could leap.

II

Father, there are things I never asked you,
Now the answers seem trivial.
Yet, for all your angry quiet, your shy muscular body,
What did you save by living less?
Except maybe on those solitary walks,
Hearing the rustle of your beloved ocean
Which never cried for an answer,
Or beat at you with insatiate fists.

III

I think of your swallowed angers,
The pain on your face when I twisted grammar.
All your life you wrestled with fears that would not
  become angels;
Inside your crabbed masculinity, was a motherly sweet-
  ness
You could let out only when you were alone,
With the damp sand under your feet, the foaming waves
  beside you.
With an artistry I still marvel at,
You remade yourself in that lonely space,
As you have remade yourself in me.

DAVID IGNATOW

A REQUIEM

My father listening to opera, that's me,
my legs outstretched upon the bed
as I lean back in my chair. I think of him
in his chair, legs crossed carelessly
and with his musing smile recalling his first wish,
to become a baritone, his smile seeking
after his youth or watching it in the distant past,
untouchable. I am alone, and the opera playing
heightens my loneliness, without son, without father,
without past or present, and my future a problem.

Eh, father, as I listen to your favorite opera
you would have enjoyed my listening and approved
emphatically, while I'd withhold myself,
tentative towards opera, as other matters burned in me,
such as the need to be free,
and so we would argue but soon fall silent
and go our separate ways.

I am alone in my apartment, alone as you were
without me in your last days at about my age.
I am listening to Rossini and thinking of you
affectionately, longing for your presence once more,
of course to wrestle with your character,
the game once again of independence,
but now, now in good humour
because we already know the outcome,

for I am sixty-six, going on sixty-seven,
and you are forever seventy-two.
We are both old men and soon enough
I'll join you. So why quarrel again,
as if two old men could possibly settle
between them what was impossible
to settle in their early days?

8

Epilogue: Clyde Clayton King

LARRY L. KING

LARRY L. KING

There was that blindly adoring period of childhood when my father was the strongest and wisest of men. He would scare off the bears my young imagination feared as they prowled the night outside our Texas farmhouse, provide sunshine and peanut butter, make the world go away. I brought him my broken toys and my skinned knees. He did imitations of all the barnyard animals; when we boxed he saw to it that I won by knockouts. After his predawn winter milkings, shivering and stomping his numb feet while rushing to throw more wood on the fire, he warned that tomorrow morning, by gosh, he planned to laze abed and eat peach cobbler while his youngest son performed the icy chores.

He took me along when he hunted rabbits and squirrels, and on alternate Saturdays when he bounced in a horse-drawn wagon over dirt roads to accomplish his limited commercial possibilities in Putnam or Cisco. He thrilled me with tales of his own small-boy peregrinations; an odyssey to Missouri, consuming two years, in covered wagons pulled by oxen; fordings of swift rivers; and pauses in Indian camps where my grandfather, Morris Miles King, smoked strong pipes with his hosts and ate with his fingers from iron kettles containing what he later called dog stew. The Old Man taught me to whistle, pray, ride a horse, enjoy country music, and, by his example, to smoke. He taught that credit buying was unmanly, unwise, and probably unforgivable in heaven; that one honored one's women, one's flag, and one's pride; that on evidence supplied by the biblical source of "winds blowing from the four corners of the earth," the world was most assuredly flat. He taught me the Old Time Religion, to bait a fishhook and gut a butchered hog. . . .

I had no way of knowing what courage was in the man (he with no education, no hope of quick riches, no visible improvements or excitements beckoning to new horizons) that permitted him to remain so cheerful, shielding, and kind. No matter how difficult those depression times, there was always something under the Christmas tree. When I was four, he walked five miles to town in a blizzard, then returned as it worsened, carrying a red rocking chair and smaller gifts in a gunnysack. Though he had violated his creed by buying on credit, he made it possible for Santa Claus to appear on time.

I would learn that he refused to accept the largess of one of FDR's recovery agencies because he feared I might be shamed or marked by wearing to school its telltale olive-drab "relief shirts." He did accept employment with the Works Progress Administration, shoveling and hauling wagonloads of dirt and gravel for a road-building project. When I brought home the latest joke from the rural school —WPA stands for We Piddle Around—he delivered a stern, voice-quavering lecture: "Son, the WPA is an honest way some poor men has of makin' their families a livin'. You'd go to bed hungry tonight without the WPA. Next time some smart aleck makes a joke about it, you ought to knock a goddamned whistlin' fart out of him."

Children learn that others have fathers with more money, more opportunity, more sophistication. Their own ambitions or resentments rise, inspiring them to reject the simpler wants of an earlier time. The son is shamed by the father's speech, dress, car, occupation, and table manners. The desire to flee the family nest (or to soar higher in it; to undertake some few experimental solos) arrives long before the young have their proper wings or before their parents can conceive of it.

The Old Man was an old-fashioned father, one who relied on corporal punishments, biblical exhortations, and a ready temper. He was not a man who dreamed much or who understood that others might require dreams as their opium. Though he held idleness to be as useless and as sinful as adventure, he had the misfortune to sire a hedonist son who dreamed of improbable conquests accomplished by some magic superior to grinding work. By the time I entered the troublesome teen-age years, we were on the way to a long, dark journey. A mutual thirst to prevail existed —some crazy stubborn infectious contagious will to avoid the slightest surrender.

The Old Man strapped, rope whipped, and caned me for smoking, drinking, lying, avoiding church, skipping school, and laying out at night. Having once been very close, we now lashed out at each other in the manner of rejected lovers on the occasion of each new disappointment. I thought The Old Man blind to the wonders and potentials of the real world; could not fathom how current events or cultural habits so vital to my contemporaries could be considered so frivolous—or worse. In turn, The Old Man expected me to obediently accept his own values: show more concern over the ultimate disposition of my eternal soul, eschew easy paths when walking tougher ones might somehow purify, be not so inquisitive or damnfool dreamy. That I could not (or would not) comply puzzled, frustrated, and angered him. In desperation he moved from a "wet" town to a "dry" one, in the foolish illusion that this tactic might keep his baby boy out of saloons.

On a Saturday in my fifteenth year, when I refused an order to dig a cesspool in our backyard because of larger plans downtown, I fought back: it was savage and ugly—though, as those things go, one hell of a good fight. But only losers emerged. After that we spoke in terse mumbles or angry shouts, not to communicate with civility for three years. The Old Man paraded to a series of punishing and uninspiring jobs—night watchman, dock loader for a creamery, construction worker, chicken butcher in a steamy, stinking poultry house, while I trekked to my own part-time jobs or to school. When school was out I usually repaired to one distant oil field or another, remaining until classes began anew. Before my eighteenth birthday I escaped by joining the Army.

On the morning of my induction, The Old Man paused at the kitchen table, where I sat trying to choke down breakfast. He wore the faded old crossed-gallus denim overalls I held in superior contempt and carried a lunch bucket in preparation of whatever dismal job then rode him. "Lawrence," he said, "is there anything I can do for you?" I shook my head. "You need any money?" "No." The Old Man shuffled uncertainly, causing the floor to creak. "Well," he said, "I wish you good luck." I nodded in the direction of my bacon and eggs. A moment later the front door slammed, followed by the grinding of gears The Old Man always accomplished in confronting even the simplest machinery.

Alone in a Fort Dix crowd of olive drab, I lay popeyed on my bunk at night, chain smoking, as Midland High School's initial 1946 football game approached. The impossible dream was that some magic carpet might transport me back to those anticipatory tingles I had known when bands blared, cheerleaders cartwheeled sweet tantalizing glimpses of their panties, and we purple-clads whooped and clattered toward the red-shirted Odessa Bronchos or the Angry Orange of San Angelo. Waste and desolation lived in the heart's private country on the night that opening game was accomplished on the happiest playing field of my forfeited youth. The next morning, a Saturday, I was called to the orderly room to accept a telegram—a form of communication that had always meant death or other disasters. I tore it open with the darkest fantasies to read MIDLAND 26 EL PASO YSLETA 0 LOVE DAD. Those valuable communiqués arrived on ten consecutive Saturday mornings.

With a ten-day furlough to spend, I appeared unannounced and before a cold dawn on the porch of that familiar frame house in Midland. The Old Man rose quickly, dispensing greetings in his woolly long-handles. "You just a first-class private?" he teased. "Lord God, I would a-thought a King would be a general by now. Reckon I'll have to write ole Harry Truman a postcard to git that straightened out." Most of the time, however (when I was not out impressing the girls with my PFC stripe), a cautious reserve prevailed. We talked haltingly, carefully, probing as uncertainly as two neophyte premed students might explore their first skin boil.

On the third or fourth day The Old Man woke me on the sleeping porch, lunch bucket in hand. "Lawrence," he said, "your mother found a bottle of whisky in your suitcase. Now, you know this is a teetotal home. We never had a bottle of whisky in a home of ours, and we been married since 19-and-11. You're perfectly welcome to stay here, but your whisky's not." I stiffly mumbled something about going to a motel. "You know better than that," The Old Man scolded. "We don't want you goin' off to no blamed motel." Then, in a weary exasperation not fully appreciated until dealing with transgressions among my own offspring: "Good God, son, what makes you want to raise ole billy hell all the time?" We regarded each other in a helpless silence. "Do what you think is right," he said, sighing. "I've done told you how me and your mother feel." He went off to work; I got up and removed the offending liquids.

The final morning brought a wet freeze blowing down from Amarillo by way of the North Pole. The Old Man's car wouldn't start; our family had never officially recognized taxis. "I'll walk you to the bus station," he said, bundling in a heavy sheepskin jumper and turning his back, I suspect, so as not to witness my mother's struggle against tears. We shivered down dark streets, past homes of my former schoolmates, by vacant lots where I played softball or slept off secret sprees, past stores I remembered for their bargains in Moon Pies and then Lucky Strikes and finally Trojans. Nostalgia and old guilts blew in with the wind. I wanted to say something healing to The Old Man, to utter some gracious good-bye (the nearest thing to retroactive apologies a savage young pride would permit), but I simply knew no beginnings.

We sat an eternity in the unreal lights of the bus station among crying babies, hung-over cowboys, and drowsing old Mexican men, in mute inspection of those dead shows provided by bare walls and ceilings. The Old Man made a silent offering of a cigarette. He was a vigorous fifty-nine then, still clear eyed, dark haired, and muscular, but as his hand extended that cigarette pack and I saw it clearly—weather cured, scarred, one finger crooked and stiff jointed from an industrial accident—I suddenly and inexplicably knew that one day The Old Man would wither, fail, die. In that moment, I think, I first sensed—if I did not understand—something of mortality; of tribes, blood, and inherited rituals.

At the door to the bus The Old Man suddenly hugged me, roughly, briefly: not certain, perhaps, such an intimacy would be tolerated by this semistranger who bore his name. His voice broke as he said, "Write us, son. We love you." I clasped his hand and brushed past, too full for words. For I knew, then, that I loved him, too, and had, even in the worst of times, and would never stop.

We took a trip last summer, one The Old Man had secretly coveted for a lifetime, though, in the end, he almost had to be prodded into the car. "I hate like the devil to leave Cora," he said of his wife of almost six decades. "She's got to where her head swims when she walks up and down the steps. She taken a bad spill just a few weeks ago. I try to stay close enough to catch her if she falls."

The Old Man did not look as if he could catch much of a falling load as he approached eighty-three. Two hundred pounds of muscle and sinew created by hard work and clean living had melted to a hundred-sixty-odd; his senior clothing flapped about him. He had not worn his bargain dentures for years, except when my mother insisted on enforcing the code of some rare social function, because, he complained, they played the devil with his gums, or gagged him, or both. The eagle's gleam was gone from eyes turned watery and rheumy; he couldn't hear so well anymore; he spoke in a wispy voice full of false starts and tuneless whistles requiring full attention.

He was thirteen years retired from his last salaried job, and he had established himself as a yard-tender and general handyman. He mowed lawns, trimmed hedges, tilled flower beds, grubbed stumps, painted houses, performed light carpentry or emergency plumbing. In his eightieth year my mother decreed that he might no longer climb trees for pruning purposes. Though he lived with that verdict, his eyes disapproved it just as they had when his sons dictated that he might no longer work during the hottest part of the desert summer days. The Old Man surrendered his vigor hard, each new concession (not driving a car or giving up cigarettes) throwing him into a restless depression. He continued to rise each morning at five, prowling the house impatiently on rainy days, muttering and growling of all the grass that needed mowing or of how far behind Midland was falling in unpainted fences. At such times he might complain because the Social Security Administration refused him permission to earn more than twelve hundred dollars annually while continuing to merit its assistance: he sneaked in more work by the simple expediency of lowering his prices. Except on the Sabbath (when, by his ethic, the normal joy of work translated to sin), he preferred the indoors only when eating or sleeping. He had long repaired to a sleeping porch of his own creation, where it was always twenty degrees cooler in winter and correspondingly hotter in the summertime; one of the curses of modernity, he held, was "refrigerated air."

On my mother's reassurances that she would spend a few days with her twin sister, we coaxed The Old Man into my car. Years earlier I had asked him whether he wanted to see some particular place or thing and whether I might take him there. To my surprise (for The Old Man had never hinted of secret passions) he said yes, he had wanted since childhood to visit the state capitol in Austin and the Alamo in San Antonio: he had read of them in books his mother had obtained when his father's death had cut off his schooling. I had long procrastinated. Living in the distant Sodoms and Gomorrahs of the East, I wandered in worlds alien to my father in search of ambitions that surely mystified him. There were flying trips home: an hour's domino playing here, an evening of conversation there. Then the desert would become too still, dark, and forbidding: I would shake his worn old hand, mutter promises and excuses, grab a suitcase; run. Last summer my wife effectively nagged me to deliver on my old pledge. And so, one boiling morning in July, we departed my father's house. He sat beside me on the front seat, shrunken and somehow remote, yet transmitting some youthful eagerness. The older he had grown, the less The Old Man had ever troubled to talk, contenting himself with sly grins or solemn stares so well timed you sometimes suspected he heard better than advertised. Deliver him a grandchild to tease and he would open up: "Bradley Clayton King, I hear turrible things on you. Somebody said you got garments on your back, and you have ancestors. And word come to me lately that you was seen hesitatin' on the doorstep." With others, however, he was slow to state his case.

Now, however, we had hardly gone a mile before The Old Man began a monologue lasting almost a week. As we roared across the desert waste, his fuzzy old voice battled with the cool cat's purr of the air conditioner; he gestured, pointed, laughed, praised the land, took on new strength.

He had a love for growing things, a Russian peasant's legendary infatuation for the motherland; for digging in the good earth, smelling it, conquering it. "Only job I ever had that could hold a candle to farmin'," he once said, "was blacksmithin'. Then the car come along, and I was blowed up." Probably his greatest disappointment was his failure as a farmer—an end dictated by depressed prices in his most productive years and hurried by land worn down through a lack of any effective application of the basic agrarian sciences. He was a walking-plow farmer, a mule-and-dray-horse farmer, a chewing-gum-and-baling-wire farmer. If God brought rain at the wrong moment, crops rotted in the mud; should He not bring it when required, they baked and died. You sowed, tilled, weeded, sweated: if heaven felt more like reward than punishment, you would not be forced to enter the Farmer's State Bank with your soiled felt hat in your hand.

World War II forced The Old Man off the family acres: he simply could not reject the seventy-odd cents per hour an oil company promised for faithful drudgery in its pipeline crew. And he felt, too, deep and simple patriotic stirrings: perhaps, if he carried enough heavy pipe quickly enough, the fall of Hitler and Tojo might be hastened. He alternately flared with temper fits and was quietly reflective on the fall day in 1942 when we quit the homestead he had come to in a covered wagon in 1894; later, receiving word of the accidental burning of that unpainted farmhouse, he walked around with tears in his eyes. He was past seventy before giving up his dream of one day returning to that embittered soil, of finally mastering it, of extracting its unkept promises. . . .

Now it was late afternoon. His sap suddenly ran low; he

seemed more fragile, a tired old head with a journey to make; he dangerously stumbled on a curbstone. Crossing a busy intersection, I took his arm. Though that arm had once pounded anvils into submission, it felt incredibly frail. My children, fueled by youth's inexhaustible gases, skipped and cavorted fully a block ahead. Negotiating the street, The Old Man half laughed and half snorted: "I recollect helpin' you across lots of streets when you was little. Never had no notion that one day you'd be doin' the same for me." Well, I said. Well. Then: "I've helped that boy up there"—motioning toward my distant and mobile son— "across some few streets. Until now, it never once occurred that he may someday return the favor." "Well," The Old Man said, "he will if you're lucky."

Three o'clock in an Austin motel. The Old Man snores in competition with jet aircraft. On an adjoining bed his grandson's measured breathing raises and lowers a pale banner of sheets. Earlier, the boy had exorcised his subconscious demons through sheet-tugging threshings and disjointed, indistinct private cries. The Old Man snores on, at peace. *Night battles never plagued me,* he once said in explaining his ability to sleep anyplace, anytime. *I never was one to worry much. What people worry about is things they can't do nothin' about. Worryin' always seemed like a waste to me. . . .*

I remembered that we had compromised our differences in about my twentieth year. My own early assumption of family responsibilities proved healing: in the natural confusions of matrimony, one soon came to appreciate The Old Man's demanding, luckless role. Nothing is so leavening to the human species as to gaze upon the new and untried flesh of another human being and realize, in a combination of humility, amazement, and fear, that you are responsible for its creation and well-being. This discovery is almost immediately followed by a sharply heightened appreciation of more senior fathers.

We discovered that we could talk again. Could even sit at ease in long and mutually cherished silence. Could civilly exchange conflicting opinions, compete in dominoes rather than in more deadly games, romp on the lawn with our descendants, and share each new family pride or disappointment. For some four years in the early 1950s we lived in close proximity. The Old Man came to accept my preference for whisky as I came to accept his distaste for what it represented; he learned to live with my skeptic's atheism as I came to live with his belief that God was as tangible an entry as the Methodist bishop.

The Old Man was sixty-six and I was twenty-five when I went away for good. There were periodic trips back home, each of them somehow more hurried, fleeting, and blurred. Around 1960 it dawned on me that The Old Man and his sons had, in effect, switched roles. On a day I cannot name, he suddenly and wordlessly passed the family crown. Now the sons were solicited for advice or leadership and would learn to live uneasily in the presence of a quiet and somehow deeply wrenching paternal deference. (*Weldon, you reckon it would be all right if I got a better car?* Well, now, dad, I believe I'd go slow on that. Maybe you don't see and hear well enough to drive in traffic very much. *Lawrence, what would you say to me and your mother goin' back to the farm?* Now, dad, why in the world? People have been starving off those old farms for fifty years. What would you do out there in the sticks, miles from a doctor, if you or mother got sick?)

The heart of the young blacksmith continued to beat in that shrinking frame, however. He could not drive a car anymore; he nodded off in the middle of the sermon at Asbury Methodist; meddlers had barred him from climbing trees. He remained very much his own man, however, in vital areas. Living by his sweat, The Old Man saved an astonishing amount of his paltry pensions and earnings, fiercely guarded his independence, took pride in his age, seldom rode when he could walk, tended the soil, ate well, and slept regularly.

On that motel bed slept a man who, at age twelve, had fallen heir to the breadwinner's role for a shotgun-widowed mother and eight younger siblings. He had accepted that burden, had discharged it without running off to sea: had drawn on some simple rugged country grace and faith permitting him no visible resentments then or later. He had sweated two family broods through famines and floods, Great Depressions and World Wars, industrial and sociological revolutions. Though a child of another century, really, he walked through the chaos and tediums of his time determinedly—as Faulkner wrote of women passing through grief and trouble—"able to go through them and come out on the other side."

The faintest dawn showed through the windows when The Old Man sat up in bed, yawning: "Lord God, is it dinnertime? Must be, you bein' awake!" He examined my face: "Didn't you get no sleep?" Some. "How much?" Three or four hours, I lied. "You ain't gonna live to see fifty," The Old Man predicted. "What you ought to do is buy you a cotton farm and work it all day. I bet you'd sleep at night, then."

He almost hopped into his trousers from a standing position, amazingly agile in that fresh hour he most cherished. Noting my inspection he asked, "Reckon you can do that at eighty-two?" Hell, I said, I can't do it at forty-one. The Old Man celebrated this superiority with a pleased grin. The previous night he had insisted on playing dominoes past midnight in the home of a favorite nephew, Lanvil Gilbert, talking it up like a linebacker: *Say you made five? Why, that makes me so mad I'll play my double-five—and gimme fifteen while you got your marker handy. . . . I forgot to tell you boys I run a domino school on the side. Got a beginner's class you might be able to git in.* Back at the motel he had again explored the distant past until his grandchildren yawned him to bed. *Old Man,* I thought, *what is the secret? What keeps you interested, laughing, loving each breath?* I remembered his enthusiastic voice on the telephone when I told him I had given my son his middle name: "I'm puttin' a five-dollar bill in the mail to buy him his first pair of long pants. Put it up and keep it. I want that exact five-dollar bill to pay for my namesake's first long pants." Grand satisfactions had visited his face earlier on our Austin trip when my son brought him a gigantic three-dollar pocket watch. The boy had shoved it at him—"Here, granddad, this is for you, I bought it out of my allowance"—and then had moved quickly away from the dangers of sentimental thanks and unmanly hugs.

As we started down to breakfast, The Old Man said, "Why don't we take Bradley Clayton with us?" Sure, if he wants to go. The Old Man gently shook the boy. "Namesake," he said. "Wake up, namesake, you sleepyhead." The boy rolled over with reluctance, blinking, trying to focus. "Git up from there," The Old Man said in feigned anger. "Time I was your age, I had milked six cows and plowed two fields by this time-a-day."

"What?" the boy said, incredulous.

"I'll make you think what!" The Old Man said, then repeated his improbable claim.

The boy, pulling his wits together, offered The Old Man a sample of the bloodline's baiting humor: "Was *that* what made you rich?"

The Old Man whooped and tousled the boy's hair, then mock-whipped him toward the bathroom.

We talked late on my final night. The Old Man sat in his jerry-built house, on a couch across from a painting of Jesus risking retina damage by looking directly into the celestial lights. Pictures of his grandchildren were on the walls and on the television top, along with a needlework replica of the Dead Kennedys appearing to hover over the U.S. Capitol, and a Woolworth print depicting a highly sanitized village blacksmith. One of his sons, thinking to please The Old Man, had given him the latter: while he appreciated the thought, he had been amused by the artist's concept. "Lord-a-mercy," he had chuckled, "the feller that painted that thing never *seen* a horse shod or a blacksmith shop either one." The painting revealed a neat, sweatless man effortlessly bending a horseshoe as he worked in an imposing brick edifice surrounded by greenery, while little girls in spotless dresses romped happily among gleaming anvils possibly compounded of sterling silver. The Old Man enjoyed comparing it with the realities of a photo made in the 1920s, showing him grease stained and grimy in a collapsing wooden structure filled with indescribable debris.

His hands—always vital to his lip movements—swooped and darted, described arcs, pointed, performed slow or vigorous dances according to the moment's chin music. Just before bed I asked in a private moment whether he had any major regrets. "Two," he said. "I wish I could of done better financially by your mother. I never meant for her to have such a hard life. And I wish I could of went to school."

On the morning of my departure he was spry and fun filled. Generally such leave-takings were accomplished in tensions and gloom; for a decade the unspoken thought had hovered that this might be the final good-bye. Last July, however, that melancholy tune was but faintly heard: The Old Man was so vigorously alive that I began to think of him as a sure centenarian. I left him standing on the front porch, wearing his workman's clothes, shaking a friendly fist against what he would do if I didn't write my mother more often.

Six weeks later he gathered a generous mess of turnip greens from his backyard vegetable garden, presenting them to his wife with the request that she concoct her special corn bread. A few hours after his meal he became dizzy and nauseated. "I just et too many of them turnip greens," he explained to his wife. Persuaded to the hospital for examinations and medications, he insisted on returning home on the grounds he had never spent a night in a hospital bed and was too old to begin. The next morning, in great pain, he consented to again be loaded into my brother's car.

The Old Man mischievously listed his age as sixteen with a crisp hospital functionary filling out the inevitable forms. He ordered nurses out when a doctor appeared, extracting a promise from my brother that "no womenfolk" would be permitted to intimately attend him. When the examining physician pressed his lower abdomen, The Old Man jerked and groaned. "Is that extremely sore, Mr. King?" Well, yes, it was a right-smart sore. "How long has it been that way?" About ten days, he reckoned. "Why didn't you tell me?" my exasperated brother inquired. The old eyes danced through the pain: "Wouldn't a done no good, you not bein' no doctor."

He consented to stay in the hospital, though he did complain that his lawn mower and supporting tools had been carelessly abandoned: would my brother see that they were locked in the backyard toolshed? Then he shook my brother's hand: "Weldon, thank you for everything." He shortly lapsed into the final chills and fevers, and before I could reach home he was gone. I saw him in his final sleep and now cannot forget those magnificently weathered old hands. They told the story of a countryman's life in an eloquent language of wrinkles, veins, old scars and new. The Old Man's hands always bore some fresh scratch or cut as adornment, the result of his latest tangle with a scrap of wire, a rusted pipe, a stubborn root; in death they did not disappoint even in that small and valuable particular. No, it is not given to sons to know everything of their fathers —mercifully, perhaps—but I have those hands in my memory to supply evidence of the obligations he met, the sweat he gave, the honest deeds performed. I like to think that you could look at those hands and read the better part of The Old Man's heart.

Clyde Clayton King lived eighty-two years, seven months, and twenty-five days. His widow, four of five children, seven of eight grandchildren, six great-grandchildren, and two great-great-grandchildren survive. His time extended from when "kissin' wasn't took lightly" to exhibitions of group sex; from five years before men on horseback rushed to homestead the Cherokee Strip to a year beyond man's first walk on the moon; from a time when eleven of twelve American families existed on average annual incomes of $380 to today's profitable tax-dodging conglomerates; from the first presidency of Grover Cleveland to the midterm confusions of Richard Nixon. Though he had plowed oxen in yoke, he never flew in an airplane. He died owing no man and knowing the satisfaction of having built his own house.

I joined my brother and my son in gathering and locking away The Old Man's tools in that backyard shed he had concocted of scrap lumbers, chipped bricks, assorted tins, and reject roofing materials. Then, each alone with his thoughts, we moved in a concert of leaky garden hose and weathered sprinklers, lingering to water his lawn.

ABOUT THE CONTRIBUTORS

Robert Alan Aurthur was a screenwriter, playwright and producer. He received two Academy Award nominations for his work on *All That Jazz*.

Joe David Bellamy has published fiction, poetry and anthologies. He is Director of the Literature Program, National Endowment for the Arts.

Clark Blaise is director of the International Writing Program at the University of Iowa. He has published short story collections, novels, and works of nonfiction.

Michael Blumenthal teaches poetry at Harvard University. He is the author of several books of poetry.

Robert Bly is a poet, storyteller, and lecturer. His book *Iron John* stirred widespread interest in men's issues.

John Ed Bradley is a novelist and free-lance writer for magazines. He is a former *Washington Post* reporter.

Brock Brower has published articles, short stories, novels and a children's book. He helped originate the television programs "20/20" and "3-2-1 Contact!"

Anatole Broyard was a critic, essayist and short story writer. He was a longtime staff member of the *New York Times*.

Jimmy Carter is a former President of the United States.

Raymond Carver published several collections of short fiction and poetry. He taught writing at a number of universities.

John Cheever was a novelist and short story writer. *The Stories of John Cheever* won a Pulitzer Prize for fiction.

Peter Clark is a copy editor for the *San Diego Union-Tribune*. He previously worked as an attorney.

James P. Comer is Professor of Child Psychiatry at the Yale University Child Study Center and Associate Dean of the Yale School of Medicine. He has published several books, many magazine articles, and writes a column for *Parents* magazine.

Rich Cowles is completing a memoir about being a father of four. His articles have appeared nationally in newspapers and magazines.

Harry Crews has published novels, short stories and works of nonfiction. He is Professor of English at the University of Florida.

James A. Cunningham is a family physician in Kentucky. He has taught at Southern Connecticut State University.

James Dickey is a poet and novelist. He is Professor of English and Poet-in-Residence at the University of South Carolina.

Ivan Doig has published novels and works of nonfiction, including a memoir of his early life in Montana. Prior to becoming a full-time writer he worked as a ranch hand, journalist and magazine editor.

Craig Donegan is a writer and columnist for the *San Antonio Express-News.* He has been a college teacher, speech-writer and free-lance contributor to magazines.

Robert Drake is Professor of English at the University of Tennessee in Knoxville. Collections of his short stories and critical essays have been published.

Stanley Elkin has published several novels and a collection of essays.

Frederick Exley is the author of three novel-memoirs which began with *A Fan's Notes.* He also writes for magazines.

Edward Field has published several books of poetry. He is editing the works of Alfred Chester.

Ronald Forsythe is the nom de plume of Donn Teal, gay historian and writer.

Nicholas Gage is the author of six books, including *Eleni,* about the murder of his mother during Greece's civil war. He is a former *New York Times* reporter.

Jim Gallagher is a reporter for the *Chicago Tribune.*

Edmund Gosse was a British Museum librarian and lecturer in English literature at Trinity College, Cambridge. Among more than twenty books, he wrote the classic memoir *Father and Son.*

Bob Greene is a *Chicago Tribune* columnist. He has published several works of nonfiction.

Joel Grey is an actor, singer and dancer. He won a Tony for his performance in the play *Cabaret,* and an Oscar for his role in the film version.

Lewis Grizzard is a nationally syndicated columnist for the *Atlanta Journal-Constitution.* He is the author of several best-selling works of nonfiction.

Christopher Hallowell has published works of nonfiction, including a memoir about his father. He has been a freelance contributor to national magazines and newspapers.

Pete Hamill is a columnist for *Esquire* and the author of several novels. He has also written several movie and television scripts.

Mike Harden is a syndicated columnist whose work has been collected in six books.

Robert Hayden taught English at the University of Michigan and was a poetry consultant to the Library of Congress. He has published several books of poetry.

James C. Hefley is Writer-in-Residence at Hannibal-LaGrange College in Hannibal, Missouri where he directs the Mark Twain Writers Conference. He is the publisher of Hannibal Books and the author of over 50 books.

Patrick Hemingway spent many years as a professional hunter and forestry officer in East Africa. He is the son of Ernest Hemingway.

Paul Hemphill is a journalist, columnist and free-lance writer for national magazines. He is the author of eight books.

Ralph Holcomb is a clinical social worker.

John Holveck is a former philosophy professor. He is currently writing a novel.

David Ignatow has published thirteen books of poetry and two of prose. He has taught at a number of universities, including the City University of New York where he is Professor Emeritus.

Pat Jordan has published several novels and works of nonfiction. He is completing a memoir about life with his father.

Larry L. King has been a congressional aide, writer, and a

Nieman Fellow at Harvard. In addition to several books he cowrote the musical comedy *The Best Little Whorehouse in Texas*.

Ronald Koertge teaches English at Pasadena City College. He has published several books of poetry and novels for young people.

Philip B. Kunhardt, Jr. is a former managing editor of *Life* magazine. He has published several works of nonfiction, including a memoir about his father.

Richard E. Lapchick is the director of Northeastern University's Center for the Study of Sport in Society.

Steve LaRue is a staff writer for the *San Diego Union-Tribune*.

Eric Lax has published several nonfiction books, including *Woody Allen: A Biography*.

Alfred Lubrano is a reporter for the *New York Daily News*. He has contributed articles to national magazines and newspapers.

Andrew H. Malcolm is national affairs correspondent for the *New York Times*. He is the author of a memoir about his mother.

Frederick Manning has written for *Reader's Digest*.

Steve Marcus is a sports reporter and columnist for *Newsday*.

Michel Marriott is a *New York Times* reporter.

George Eyre Masters is a novelist and free-lance writer. He is completing a novel based on his military experience during the Vietnam War.

Joseph Mastrangelo is a former news artist and journalist. He was head cartographer and a feature writer for the *Washington Post*.

Robert Mezey is Professor of English and Poet-in-Residence at Pomona College. He has published several books of poetry.

Lance Morrow is a senior writer for *Time* magazine. He is the author of a memoir about his father.

Bill Moyers is a television journalist for PBS. He is a former press secretary to Lyndon Johnson, publisher of *Newsday* and columnist for *Newsweek*.

Samuel Osherson is a research psychologist and practicing psychotherapist. He teaches at the Fielding Institute and has been a faculty member at Harvard, MIT and the University of Massachusetts.

Dean Pitchford is a screenwriter and an Academy Award–winning lyricist.

David Plante is the author of several novels.

David S. Powell is Lifestyle Editor of the *Indianapolis Star* and a free-lance writer.

Burt Prelutsky has been a *Los Angeles Times* columnist and free-lance writer for national magazines. He has also written scripts for several television movies.

Alastair Reid is a poet, prose writer and translator. A long-time staff writer for *The New Yorker,* he has published over twenty books.

Theodore Roethke was a poet and faculty member of a number of universities. His book *The Waking: 1933–1953* won a Pulitzer Prize for poetry.

Jim Sanderson is a syndicated columnist and author. He has written for many national magazines.

Ralph Schoenstein is the author of many books, including a memoir about his father.

Edward Serotta is an American photojournalist who has lived in Hungary and Germany since 1988. His first book is a photographic portrait of postwar Jewish life in central Europe.

Gary Allen Sledge is a senior editor at *Reader's Digest*.

Jerry Smith owns an advertising and public relations company.

Lee Thomas is a writer of screenplays.

Lewis Thomas is scholar-in-residence at Cornell University Medical College. He is the author of several best-selling books.

Anthony Walton has published poetry, short stories and magazine articles. He is completing a book about the history of Mississippi based on his family's experiences in that state.

Irving Wexler has published several books of poetry and short stories.

Paul Wilkes is the author of eight books, two of which were the basis of documentaries he produced for PBS. He teaches writing at Clark University.

David Wojahn has published three books of poetry. He teaches at Indiana University.

Lawrence Wright is a free-lance writer for national magazines. He has published two books of nonfiction and is completing a third.

Paul Zweig was a poet, essayist, and translator. He wrote several books, and taught at universities in the United States and France.

INDEX OF CONTRIBUTORS

COPYRIGHT ACKNOWLEDGMENTS